THE ROYAL NAVY

During the last couple of years, ministers have spoken of the government's intention to build a bigger Navy, a sentiment undoubtedly shared by most of those reading this introduction. Such an expansion could easily be justified on the basis of:

- Hostility to the West expressed by Russia which is increasing its naval forces.
- A massive increase in the size of the Chinese navy, which continues to expand.
- The likelihood that in future conflicts the involvement of the USA cannot be guaranteed.
- The fact that the UK in leaving the EU will have to devote more resources to security not only in respect of our borders and coastline, but also our fisheries.
- The reintroduction of Carrier Strike, with the possibility that, from time to time, both carriers will be in service. Each will, therefore, require full surface and sub-surface protection.

What we have not been told about are the areas where such naval expansion is likely to be centred. Clearly, a "bigger Navy" must mean its frontline. It would be an absurdity if, for example, the government in building up a bigger Navy, simply increased the number of patrol boats. The present frontline (on paper) is as follows:

- Two carriers
- Six Type 45 destroyers
- Eight ASW (Anti-Submarine Warfare) Type 23 frigates
- Five general-purpose Type 23 frigates
- Two LPDs (amphibious)
- Seven SSNs (fleet submarines)
- Total 30

The actual figure is 27, on account of the following:
- Only one carrier (QUEEN ELIZABETH) is in service. Her sister-ship (PRINCE OF WALES) will commence sea trials later this year.
- Of the two LPDs (ALBION and BULWARK), it is government policy to maintain only one in service, with the other held in deep reserve, such that she could not be reactivated for many months. An additional problem would be a shortage of personnel to man a second ship.

Only six SSNs (three Trafalgars and three Astutes) are in service. However, with four Astute Class under construction, or on order, numbers will have increased to seven by 2024 when HMS AGINCOURT, the last Astute, is commissioned. Unless the government reverses its policy on numbers of LPDs in service, the Navy is unlikely to achieve a frontline of 30. Where might an expansion be seen?

HMS Kent

Carriers
It is all very well for ministers to aspire to having two operational carriers. However, taking account of essential refits, this would only be possible on a permanent basis if a third carrier was ordered. With QUEEN ELIZABETH and PRINCE OF WALES absorbing over £6bn in construction costs, a third carrier seems highly unlikely, particularly bearing in mind the state of the MoD's budget and the lack of personnel. When QUEEN ELIZABETH sailed for the USA in August 2018, she had, on board, 1500 personnel.

Destroyers
The naval staff requirement was for the 12 Type 42 destroyers to be replaced by the Type 45s on a one-for-one basis. For budgetary reasons, the number quickly fell to eight. Under Labour, this was further trimmed to six on the ridiculous basis (this was how the minister announced the decision in the Commons) that as the first of class (Daring) had proved herself to be so much more effective than envisaged, the Navy could fulfil its commitments with six instead of eight.

Members of the public were less than impressed when the MoD disclosed that the programme had cost the taxpayer over £6bn. Immediately, the press seized on this. Every time a Type 45 appeared in the news, she was described as, for example, "£1bn destroyer sails for the Gulf". What the MoD should have done was to have disclosed that the average construction cost of a Type 45 destroyer was, in fact, £633m, making this a £3.8bn investment. The remaining £2.2bn is accounted for by way of research and development costs, or, in other words, in-house overheads.

Restarting production would create many difficulties, not least the absence of specialist UK shipbuilding facilities with BAE Systems fully committed to Type 26 construction on the Clyde. It would be pointless suggesting the placing of an order for another two or three Type 45s with a European shipyard, as it is government policy that specialised warships can only be constructed in the UK.

ASW frigates
There are presently eight ASW Type 23 frigates in service. Originally, it had been planned that all 13 Type 23s would be replaced by the Type 26 on a one-for-one basis. Indeed, we were assured by a former First Sea Lord (throughout his tenure in office) that this was government policy. Then came the bombshell. In fact, only eight would be constructed. The other five general purpose Type 23s would be replaced by a new concept, namely the Type 31e frigate which would be designed with an eye to the potential export market.

No one in government has ever explained why numbers of Type 26 frigates were cut by five. The prime suspect is the Treasury, which exercises enormous influence over government procurement policy. Mind you, you could hardly blame the Treasury for balking at the price to be paid to BAE Systems for the first three – a colossal £3.7bn. That works out at an astonishing £1233m per frigate. Of course, there will be some research and development costs featuring within that figure. Nevertheless, compared with what other nations are spending on new frigates, the price quoted by BAE Systems takes some explaining.

The other factor which militates against a class of more than eight is the leisurely construction programme agreed between BAE Systems and the MoD. The first of class (on which construction commenced a good 18 months ago) will not be in service until the mid-2020s (or even later). Only one frigate can be constructed at any time. The proposed frigate construction hall at Govan which would have cost £200m (a pittance) and which would have enabled two Type 26 frigates to be constructed, under cover, simultaneously, never passed the planning stage. Nevertheless, can you blame BAE Systems for not wanting to build the construction hall if the ultimate order was for only eight ships? Ironically, the Type 26 looks as if it will generate export sales with Australia committed and Canada interested.

General-purpose frigates

With no more carriers, Type 45s or Type 26s likely, the Navy's great white hope is that the Type 31e will go into serious production for both the home and export markets. Nevertheless, ministers stoically repeat that there will be a minimum of five Type 31es ordered for the Navy. They won't commit to a greater number.

Presently, there are two major issues. Firstly, the invitation to tender which went out last year, was subsequently withdrawn due to the subsequent absence of competitive bids. The process has been started again. Secondly, the price tag (presumably another Treasury intervention) has been put at the absurdly low figure of £250m per frigate. Compare that with a Type 26 frigate. Could any shipbuilder construct a Type 31 for just £250m and, if they could, are they likely to make any profit? Again, there would be no question of building Type 31es for the Navy in a continental shipyard. It is also dubious whether the UK's few remaining shipbuilders would have the capacity to construct Type 31es in any great number.

LPDs

Over the last 12 months, serious concern has been expressed about the real possibility of the government axing either ALBION or BULWARK. Fortunately, sense has prevailed and both will be retained. Equally, it remains troubling that the government gave such an idea any thought at all. This does not auger well for the future when in the early 2030s, the LPDs will need replacement. There is talk of a class of LHDs (i.e. having the docking facilities of an LPD and the helicopter facilities of an LPH). The Navy lost its last LPH when HMS OCEAN was sold to Brazil a year or so ago for a derisory £65m.

Perhaps the MoD might convince ministers that the Navy needs four LHDs to replace ALBION, BULWARK and, technically, OCEAN, with one in refit/reserve. But in any event, it will be at least ten years before there is any real development on this front. Already, there is a school of thought questioning the need for such large ships in the future providing amphibious capabilities.

SSNs

Perhaps ministers are thinking in terms of a naval expansion beneath the waves. As repeated a number of times by the NAO, there is a naval staff requirement for an eighth Astute-class SSN. However, the government has shown no interest in this. Policy is to build seven Astutes and no more. Again, the dead hand of the Treasury is never far from the table. But at £1675m per boat, we do need to give careful consideration as to how precious defence resources should be spent.

A further factor is the replacement programme for the Vanguard-class SSBNs - the nuclear deterrent. Parliament is largely united in its support of this multi-billion-pound programme. As already mentioned, the Astute programme will complete in 2024. BAE Systems Barrow will then be able to devote its energies to the construction of the four-boat Dreadnought Class, of which work has already commenced on HMS DREADNOUGHT.

It is possible to squeeze an eighth Astute into the programme, but only at the expense of delaying the Dreadnought Class. As it is, the Vanguards will have to remain in service for much longer than designed. Delays are likely to be resisted by all interested parties. And, of course, an eighth Astute will cost £1675m. Where is that money to be found?

An expanded Navy does seem to be a distant dream, unlikely to be achieved until the 2030s or later. The best that can be hoped would be additional numbers of Type 31es over and above the five presently planned.

Where does the Navy stand at the beginning of 2019 and what problems lie ahead? The most serious concerns relate to money and manpower. You cannot build ships without money and even if that was available, they cannot go to sea (as we found last year with the Type 23 frigate HMS IRON DUKE) without trained personnel.

Money
NATO has decreed that all its members should strive to spend 2% of GDP on defence. The UK is just one of five members that has achieved the target of 2%. However, there are many who have argued that the UK has only hit the 2% minimum by way of creative accounting, namely transferring commitments, such as pensions, from one department to the MoD.

It is true that the Chancellor of the Exchequer found an additional £800m for defence in the year to March 2019 and has promised an extra £1bn for defence in the year to March 2020. The defence budget for 2018/19 is £42.6bn or 2.12% of GDP. The Commons Defence Committee wants defence spending to increase to 3% of GDP, which would amount to an additional £16bn per annum. Former Defence Secretary Sir Michael Fallon and Defence Minister Tobias Ellwood, want an increase to 2.5%. Nevertheless, the Defence Committee received expert evidence to the effect that a 2.5% target would only be enough to catch up, namely eliminate the shortfall in spending on procurement (see below). The problem stems from the MoD having grand plans for procurement across all three Services, over the next ten years. However, the reality is that the money simply isn't there and won't be there in the future when the bills begin to roll in.

This has been brought to the attention of the MoD by the Commons Defence Committee, the Public Accounts Committee and the National Audit Office on a regular basis. In its report published at the end of January 2019, the Public Accounts Committee again castigated the MoD over its procurement budget. For the period April

HMS Montrose

2018 to March 2028 inclusive, the MoD plans to spend £193bn on equipment and support costs. However, the budget is just £186bn, leaving a shortfall of £7bn. The MoD accepts that the shortfall could eventually amount to £15bn. As the Committee chairman said at the launch of the report: *"The MoD's progress with addressing the concerns set out in our last report... has been woeful."*

Does the MoD believe that, suddenly, like a knight on a white charger, the Treasury will come to its rescue and deliver a fat cheque? Or, as it has confirmed as a possibility, will some procurement projects have to be axed? Not much scope there for lots of additional Type 31e frigates. Realistically, even an extra three would cost the Treasury another £1bn.

Joint Strike Fighter
The F-35B Joint Strike Fighter looks increasingly likely to be the obvious candidate for a partial axe. The government is committed to purchasing 138 JSFs. Hitherto, the intention was to acquire the F-35B (a jump-jet) solely for the purpose of operating from the Queen Elizabeth-class carriers. However, these aircraft will be "owned" by the RAF and acquired out of its budget. The RAF loses its remaining Tornado jets in March 2019. That will leave it solely dependent upon the Eurofighter as its only combat jet. However, the JSF, a fifth-generation fighter, is more advanced than Eurofighter.

The land-based version of the JSF (the F-35A) is a conventional aircraft, i.e. not a jump-jet. The RAF is keen to acquire it. It is also cheaper than the F-35B.

The planned inventory for the Queen Elizabeth Class is 24 F-35Bs, plus some 16 helicopters. The contract for the first batch of 48 aircraft at a cost of £9bn has been signed. This works out at £190m per aircraft. The actual construction cost of an F-35B is about £80m. The other £110m is accounted for in respect of support, maintenance and training. This is an astonishingly high figure.

It was recently announced that Lockheed Martin (who construct the JSF) and the US Department of Defense have agreed that by 2020, the construction cost of the F-35A will have been reduced to £61.5m per aircraft.

Accordingly, it will cost three quarters that of the F-35B, to acquire the F-35A. This will not go unnoticed by the Treasury. If the first 48 are costing £9bn, it would seem likely that the remaining 90 will cost another £17bn. Frankly, this is unaffordable. It seems inevitable that few of the remaining 90 will ever be acquired.

On the one hand, the Navy will insist that these 90 should be the F-35B variant. On the other, the RAF will, not unreasonably, point out that opting for the F-35A instead (which cannot operate from the Queen Elizabeth Class) would be far cheaper.

If it succeeds with this argument, the RAF gets the second batch at the expense of the Navy. That then leaves just 48 F-35Bs (nine have been delivered to date) available for carrier operations. With a substantial number needed for training (at least a squadron of 12), you would never get more than 18 available for service on each carrier, if that.

The writing is on the wall. The Navy needs to seize the initiative. It must suggest to ministers that the second batch should be another 24 F-35Bs and that the remaining 66 be axed. It would then have 60 for operation on the two carriers, together with a training squadron of 12.

Furthermore, the Navy cannot make up numbers by acquiring the far cheaper Super Hornet (in service with the US Navy) instead as it requires "cats-and-traps", i.e. arrester wires for landing, something with which the Queen Elizabeth Class will never be retrofitted, due to the enormous expense.

As a retired admiral said in a recent letter to a national daily, the UK is in grave danger of ending up with either insufficient aircraft or no aircraft available for operation on two highly expensive carriers.

Furthermore, it is conceivable that the RAF may not always be in a position (or willing) to make its F-35Bs available to the Navy, simply because someone has decided to put QUEEN ELIZABETH or PRINCE OF WALES to sea and has asked for a squadron or two to be flown down to Portsmouth from RAF Marham in Norfolk. It was recently reported that the RAF is keen to deploy the F-35B to Cyprus for operations in the Near East. Conflict between the two services seems inevitable.

The MoD insists that the shortfall in its procurement budget can be addressed. It is confident that the answer is by finding efficiency savings. However, as one recently retired First Sea Lord said in an interview, he had spent most of his career finding efficiency savings. The savings barrel, in his opinion, was now completely empty.

The financial crisis facing the MoD cannot be addressed by any one of the following factors:
- A modest increase in defence spending
- The abandonment of one or two defence programmes
- Identifying efficiency savings

The solution is to be found in relation to the funding of the MoD's biggest spending programme to date, namely the 'Successor'.

The Successor is the programme for the replacement of the UK's four Vanguard-class ballistic missile submarines (SSBNs) – Britain's nuclear deterrent. Vanguard and her three sister-boats are due for replacement in ten to 15 years' time. The £41bn programme has already commenced.

The Successor is already sucking in excess of at least £4bn per annum from the defence budget. It was George Osborne (former Chancellor) who decided that the MoD should pay for the Successor out of its own budget.

Both previous programmes, namely Polaris (the Resolution Class) and Trident (the Vanguard Class) had been funded by the Treasury from outside the defence budget.

To add to the MoD's agony, neither Osborne, nor Hammond (his successor) have ploughed additional funding into the defence budget specifically to pay for the Successor – in other words, a double whammy.

The only realistic solution to the MoD's financial woes is for Gavin Williamson, the Defence Secretary, to tell Philip Hammond that he either funds the Successor from outside the defence budget, or he will resign. There seems little prospect of either of these events from happening.

If Hammond agreed, most of the MoD's problems would disappear. The funding gap would be removed. The government could then begin to plan for a bigger Navy, as opposed to continuing with what has become a process of wishful thinking. If Hammond declines, it seems inevitable that funding for the Successor will swamp the MoD's budget for the next ten to 15 years and as a consequence, many procurement programmes will either be scrapped or deferred. Furthermore, until the Successor programme has been completed, there seems little chance of a bigger Navy.

A few years ago, a serving Minister of State for the Armed Forces warned me that if the Successor programme was given the go-ahead, it would be at the expense of the surface fleet. How right he was.

ASW
As Secretary of State for Defence, Williamson admitted to the Commons Defence Committee, last year, that there had been a tenfold increase in Russian submarine activity in the North Atlantic. In one of its reports, the Defence Committee said that a marked increase in Russian naval activity in UK waters was of concern to the government. The Defence Committee believes that the most serious maritime issue is the need for greater ASW capability. How would this be addressed?

The government could revert to its original intention of building 13 Type 26 ASW frigates. The number of Type 23 frigates was originally 16. Some 15 years ago, three of them were decommissioned and sold to the Chilean navy. Perhaps, therefore, we need a class of 16 Type 26 frigates to address the ASW crisis.

The government could order more Astute-class SSNs, but only at the expense of and by delaying the Successor programme, which seems most unlikely. It should be noted that the Astute Class, together with the US navy Virginia Class, are regarded as the most advanced fleet submarines in the world. When HMS ASTUTE entered service, the Americans were awestruck.

It has been suggested to the Commons Defence Committee that the number of P-8A Poseidon ASW aircraft being acquired for the RAF (just nine) is grossly inadequate and that there should be at least 16.

Personnel
The Strategic Defence and Security Review of 2015 provided for a target of 30,450 naval personnel (including Royal Marines) by 2025. It had been hoped that that figure

would be reached well before that date. However, present indications are that this will not be achieved until 2022 at the earliest. As at January 2018, the Navy's personnel amounted to 29,300, a shortfall of 1,150 on target.

Vice Admiral Tony Radakin (then Second Sea Lord) told the Commons Defence Committee last year that the number of engineering technicians had increased and that the outflow of skilled personnel had been reduced. He went on to say that the Submarine Service was getting back to normal with regard to personnel, but that the situation remained stressful and needed to be improved.

Morale in the armed forces continues to be low (67%), compared with just 33% in 2010. Those volunteering to leave the armed forces increased from 3.8% in March 2010 to 5.6% in December 2017.

The latest statistics indicate that the Navy is 16% below its recruitment target. Accordingly, problems remain not only with regard to retention, but also recruitment.

Pay was increased by 2.9% in July 2018, adding another £200m per annum to the defence budget. Nevertheless, no new money was put into defence in order to accommodate this increase.

It seems remarkable that a country with a population of 66 million cannot manage to employ 30,000 personnel for service in its navy and marines. In comparison, the USA with a population of 326 million, employs 363,000 in the US navy and marines. With just five times the population, the US naval forces employ 12½ times the number of people presently serving in the Royal Navy.

Conclusion

One should not conclude from this that the situation is all doom and gloom. There is much to be positive about. QUEEN ELIZABETH has already demonstrated that she will, in the future, prove to be a major asset not only for the UK, but also for NATO. In just two years' time, she will start her first operational deployment. The F-35B is gradually coming into service and is already being described as far superior to any other military aircraft being flown today.

Problems in relation to the propulsion system for the Type 45 destroyers are now being addressed, albeit somewhat slowly. As for the ships themselves, many of the world's navies regard the Type 45s with envy.

The Type 23s remain the workhorse of the Fleet. They are being regularly modernised with the latest equipment.

The Astute Class is gradually coming into service and is widely regarded as an outstanding ASW platform.

The Navy's amphibious forces, together with the Royal Marines, continue to provide sterling service.

The Merlin and Wildcat helicopters are highly regarded and will continue to serve on carriers, destroyers, frigates and auxiliaries.

The Navy's personnel are, undoubtedly, the best in the world.

Money and manpower remain the two key problems, which this government must now urgently address.

Christopher Cope
Parliamentary Correspondent Warship World (1992-2019)
Winner of the Maritime Foundation's Desmond Wettern Award
for Best Journalism (2018)
March 2018

LOCKHEED MARTIN   **HMS Queen Elizabeth**

SHIPS OF THE ROYAL NAVY
Pennant Numbers

Ship	P. No.	Page	Ship	P. No.	Page
Aircraft Carriers			**Submarines**		
QUEEN ELIZABETH	R08	19	VANGUARD	S28	14
PRINCE OF WALES	*R09*	*19*	VICTORIOUS	S29	14
			VIGILANT	S30	14
Assault Ships			VENGEANCE	S31	14
			TRENCHANT	S91	17
ALBION	L14	21	TALENT	S92	17
BULWARK	L15	21	TRIUMPH	S93	17
			ASTUTE	S94	15
Destroyers			ARTFUL	S95	15
			AMBUSH	S96	15
DARING	D32	22	*AUDACIOUS*	*S97*	*15*
DAUNTLESS	D33	22	*ANSON*	*S98*	*15*
DIAMOND	D34	22	*AGAMEMNON*	*S99*	*15*
DRAGON	D35	22	*AGINCOURT*	*S100*	*15*
DEFENDER	D36	22			
DUNCAN	D37	22	**Minehunters**		
			LEDBURY	M30	27
Frigates			CATTISTOCK	M31	27
			BROCKLESBY	M33	27
KENT	F78	24	MIDDLETON	M34	27
PORTLAND	F79	24	CHIDDINGFOLD	M37	27
SUTHERLAND	F81	24	HURWORTH	M39	27
SOMERSET	F82	24	PENZANCE	M106	29
ST ALBANS	F83	24	PEMBROKE	M107	29
LANCASTER	F229	26	GRIMSBY	M108	29
ARGYLL	F231	26	BANGOR	M109	29
IRON DUKE	F234	26	RAMSEY	M110	29
MONMOUTH	F235	26	BLYTH	M111	29
MONTROSE	F236	26	SHOREHAM	M112	29
WESTMINSTER	F237	24			
NORTHUMBERLAND	F238	24			
RICHMOND	F239	24			

Entries displayed in lighter typeface have yet to be completed

HMS Vengeance

SUBMARINES
VANGUARD CLASS

Ship	Pennant Number	Completion Date	Builder
VANGUARD	S28	1992	VSEL
VICTORIOUS	S29	1994	VSEL
VIGILANT	S30	1997	VSEL
VENGEANCE	S31	1999	VSEL

Displacement: 15,980 tonnes (submerged) **Dimensions:** 149.9m x 12.8m x 12m **Machinery:** 1 x Rolls-Royce PWR2 nuclear reactor; 2 GEC Turbines, 27,500 hp; single shaft; pump jet propulsor; two auxiliary retractable propulsion motors **Speed:** 25 + submerged **Armament:** 16 Tubes for Lockheed Trident 2 (D5) missiles, 4 Torpedo Tubes **Complement:** 135 (14 officers)

Notes: These four submarines form the UK's strategic nuclear deterrent force. Each Strategic Missile Submarine is armed with Trident 2 D5 nuclear missiles. HMS Vanguard was the first to carry out a Trident missile test firing in May 1994. She was also the first to operate a deterrent patrol in 1995 which has been maintained ever since. They are based at Faslane, Scotland, and each boat has two captains and two crews, which means the duty crew are out while their opposite numbers are at base to train or take leave. The UK's Trident missiles have been de-targeted since 1994 and the submarine is normally at several days notice to fire her missiles. The service life of the submarines have been extended to beyond 2028 while at the same time reducing the number of operational missiles on each submarine to just eight. To achieve the 5 year extension three additional Long Overhaul Periods will be required between 2014 and 2024 costing around £1.3 billion. Sensitive sonar enable them to hear vessels over 50 miles away.

HMS Astute

ASTUTE CLASS

Ship	Pennant Number	Completion Date	Builder
ASTUTE	S94	2007	BAe Submarine Solutions
AMBUSH	S96	2012	BAe Submarine Solutions
ARTFUL	S95	2015	BAe Submarine Solutions
AUDACIOUS	*S97*	*2018*	*BAe Submarine Solutions*
ANSON	*S98*	*2020*	*BAe Submarine Solutions*
AGAMEMNON	*S99*	*2022*	*BAe Submarine Solutions*
AGINCOURT	*S100*	*2024*	*BAe Submarine Solutions*

Displacement: 7,400 tonnes (7,800 tonnes submerged) **Dimensions:** 97m x 11.2m x 9.5m **Machinery:** Rolls-Royce PWR2; 2 Alsthom Turbines, 27,500 hp; single shaft; pump jet propulsor; two motors for emergency drive; one auxiliary retractable propeller **Speed:** 29+ submerged **Armament:** 6 Torpedo Tubes; Spearfish torpedoes; Tomahawk cruise missiles for a payload of 38 weapons **Complement:** 110 (including 12 Officers)

Notes: Ordered in 1997, the Astute Class will replace the Trafalgar Class in RN service. In February 2016 ARTFUL test fired her first torpedo using the BAE Systems designed Common Combat System (CCS), which functions as the digital 'brain' of the boat controlling its 'eyes', 'ears' and 'nervous system.' Using the torpedo test, the system was able to interpret sonar readings, and then attack a moving target with a practice weapon. The CCS, completed ahead of time so it was ready for the third rather than fourth Astute submarine, uses the latest technology to collect and process huge amounts of data from sensors such as sonar, providing key information to help inform important Command decisions.

The Astute Class is designed to fulfil a range of key strategic and tactical roles including anti-ship and anti-submarine operations, surveillance and intelligence gathering and support for land forces. Each boat will have a lock in lock out capability, enabling swimmers to leave the submarine while dived. This capability is in addition to the Chalfont dry deck hangar which can be fitted to the aft casing and designed to hold a swimmer delivery vehicle for stand off insertion.

The fourth boat, AUDACIOUS, was launched on 28 April 2017, being lowered into the dock water for the first time to begin the next phase of its test and commissioning programme ahead of leaving Barrow for sea trials in 2018. In January 2018 she achieved a significant milestone when she successfully completed her first dive. Known as a 'trim and basin dive' the event took place at BAE Systems' Devonshire Dock at Barrow-in-Furness. The operation saw the high-tech submarine submerge fully under water for the first time, enabling the mixed Royal Navy, Ministry of Defence and BAE Systems team on board to test many of the vessel's systems. Some 16 tonnes of lead were taken on board and moved across the width of the vessel so naval architects could confirm their calculations. The crew then dived 15m underwater to prove the safety and sta-bility of the 7,400 tonnes, 97m-long attack submarine.

In November 2015 the MoD awarded a contract for the delivery of ANSON, taking the total value for work on the vessel to £1.3 billion. The full contract covers the design and remaining build, test and commissioning activities on ANSON. Manufacturing com-menced in 2010 and is on schedule to leave for sea trials in 2020.

In April 2017 the MoD announced a further £1.4 billion for the construction of the sixth boat, AGAMEMNON, which began in 2012. In July 2017 ASTUTE returned to the fleet after completing a major capability upgrade and a sea training period.

As a matter of record the previously announced planned in-service dates for the remainder of the Astute Class boats are: AUDACIOUS (2018); ANSON (2020); AGAMEM-NON (2022) and AGINCOURT* (2024).

*Last year we wrote that there was some confusion as to whether or not the seventh boat would be named AJAX. The name has been associated with the Astute class for some years and has appeared both in print and on the RN website, but this was removed early 2018. Whether or not the name was released unofficially or has fallen out of favour was unknown and there was growing concern that Hull 7 remained unfunded and that it could fall victim to future defence cuts. But on 6 March 2018 defence procurement minister Guto Bebb confirmed that the MoD had gained Treasury approval to sign a contract for Astute Boat 7.

In May 2018, Defence Secretary Gavin Williamson confirmed that the seventh Astute-class nuclear submarine would be named HMS AGINCOURT and would have provision for up to 38 weapons in six 21-inch torpedo tubes. The submarine will be capable of using Tomahawk Block IV land-attack missiles with a range of 1,000 miles and Spearfish heavyweight torpedoes. It is now understood that construction of the sev-enth submarine has started.

HMS Triumph

TRAFALGAR CLASS

Ship	Pennant Number	Completion Date	Builder
TRENCHANT	S91	1988	Vickers
TALENT	S92	1990	Vickers
TRIUMPH	S93	1991	Vickers

Displacement: 4,500 tonnes (5,298 tonnes submerged) **Dimensions:** 85.4m x 9.8m x 9.5m **Machinery:** Rolls-Royce PWR1; 2 GEC Turbines, 15,000 hp; single shaft; pump jet propulsor; one motor for emergency drive - retractable propeller **Speed:** 30+ dived **Armament:** 5 Torpedo Tubes; Spearfish torpedoes; Tomahawk cruise missiles for a payload of 24 weapons **Complement:** 130

Notes: Over the years all of the Trafalgar Class submarines have undergone upgrades and received Type 2076 Sonar. In 2014 they also received a communications package upgrade to overcome obsolescence issues. With delays to the Astute Class, decommissioning dates for the remaining T-class have been extended. In August 2016, TRIUMPH returned to frontline operations following a maintenance period while TRENCHANT completed an extensive maintenance period at Devonport where she received major capability upgrades to her combat system and external communications equipment. In June 2018 TALENT re-joined the frontline operational fleet after an extensive multi-million pound maintenance period at HM Naval Base Devonport in Plymouth. In April 2018 TRENCHANT broke through the ice of the North Pole with two US submarines to bring Ice Exercise 2018 to an end. TORBAY was decommissioned on 18 July 2017. The three remaining boats are scheduled to decommission as follows: TRENCHANT (2019); TALENT (2021) and TRIUMPH (2022).

HMS Queen Elizabeth

HMS Queen Elizabeth

AIRCRAFT CARRIER
QUEEN ELIZABETH CLASS

Ship	Pennant Number	Completion Date	Builder
QUEEN ELIZABETH	R08	2017	Aircraft Carrier Alliance
PRINCE OF WALES	*R09*	*2019*	*Aircraft Carrier Alliance*

Displacement: 65,500 tonnes FL **Dimensions:** 282.9m x 38.8m x 11m **Machinery:** Integrated Full Electric Propulsion; 2 RR MT30 GT alternators, 93,870 hp (70 MW), 4 Wärtsilä DG, 53,064 hp (39.6 MW); 4 induction motors, 53,640 hp (40 MW); 2 shafts **Speed:** 26 knots **Armament:** 3 x Phalanx, 4 x 30mm **Aircraft:** Up to 36 x F-35B Lightning and 4 x Merlin ASaC (Crowsnest). Typical mix could be 12-24 F-35B and various helicopters which could include Merlin, Chinook, Wildcat and Apache **Complement:** 686 + 830 Air Group

Notes: A contract for the construction of the two aircraft carriers, the largest warships to be designed and built in the UK, was signed in July 2008 between the Government and the Aircraft Carrier Alliance, an industrial group comprising BAE Systems Surface Ships, Babcock Marine, Thales and the Ministry of Defence.

The first of class QUEEN ELIZABETH began sea trials in June 2017 and was commissioned at Portsmouth on 7 December 2017. In January 2018, she sailed to undergo initial Operational Sea Training, before being taken into the North Atlantic for the first time for heavy weather trials and helicopter certification operations. On return, further work prepared the ship for operation of fixed-wing aircraft. In August 2018 she was deployed to the east coast of the United States for Westlant 18 where flying trials for the F-35 Lightning begun. Joined by her task group, including HMS MONMOUTH, it marked the first time F-35 stealth jets have flown from the carrier's flight deck. As well as the vital deck trials, the deployment also involved exercises to prove the ship's ability to operate with other nations' ships and aircraft. During the Development Trials, F-35 jets conducted 202 takeoffs from the ship's ski ramp, 187 vertical landings, and 15 shipborne vertical landings - a landing technique unique to the UK. They also dropped 54 inert bombs, testing the weight loading in a variety of weather conditions and sea states. In October 2018 QUEEN ELIZABETH made a historic week-long visit to New York.During 2019 and 2020 there will be further fixed-wing trials, work-up for the embarked battle staff, and building up the carrier strike group construct.

In January 2019 she started having her Phalanx Close-In Weapons Systems (CIWS) fitted. CIWS is designed for use as an anti-aircraft and anti-missile defence. The vessel also carries 30mm Automated Small Calibre Guns and Miniguns for use against fast attack craft. The system is radar-controlled and is said to provide a "last chance" defence for ships against anti-ship missiles and aircraft.

The aircraft carrier's flight deck has to be protected from the extreme temperatures produced by the Pratt & Whitney F-135 engine fitted to the F-35Bs. A system, developed by Monitor Coatings, uses a combination of aluminium and titanium to withstand temperatures of up to 1,500°C. The high cost of the coating, and the lengthy application process, mean that it is only being applied to selected areas of the flight deck. The thermal coating is applied using a specially developed twin wire arc technique, with the powdered metal fired through a jet of plasma at temperatures of almost 10,000°C. The molten droplets then flatten and quickly solidify, creating a resilient non-skid coating that is bonded to the steel beneath. Approximately 2,000m^2 of the 19,000m^2 flight deck will be coated, comprising landing spots 2, 3 and 4, the intermediate runway between 3 and 4, and the runway spot 2 up to the 350 ft line.

Currently, construction of the PRINCE OF WALES is ahead of schedule. On 21 December 2017 she was moved from drydock to the fitting out basin. She is 3,000 tonnes heavier than her sister was at the same stage - as the second ship in the class, construction and fitting out moved more swiftly thanks to the lessons learned building QUEEN ELIZABETH. Originally planned for 2018, the 'undocking' of the carrier took place ahead of schedule and just three months after the carrier was officially named.

In November 2018 one of her four diesel engines, which are directly coupled to the generators, was powered-up for the first time marking a key milestone. The initial run of diesel generator 4 (one of two aft diesel generators) was the culmination of years of hard work. In the bowels of the carrier there are four Wärtsilä diesel generators, each capable of producing more than 11 Megawatts of power - enough to support a town of 25,000 people. In December 2018 the forward Gas Turbine Alternator (GTA) was started for the first time, three years after it was first installed on the ship and manufactured around 10 years ago. The GTA is performing as designed and ready to support the next phase of basin trials. Based on the Rolls Royce Trent 800, which were used for the Boeing 777, the MT30 is the world's most power-dense Marine Gas Turbine, a key feature for Naval Ships where high power occupying minimum space is essential. Expectations are that PRINCE OF WALES will be commissioned at the end of 2019.

HMS Albion

LANDING PLATFORM DOCK
ALBION CLASS

Ship	Pennant Number	Completion Date	Builder
ALBION	L14	2003	BAe Systems
BULWARK	L15	2004	BAe Systems

Displacement: 18,797 tonnes FL, 21,500 tonnes (flooded) **Dimensions** 176m x 28.9m x 7.1m **Machinery:** Diesel-electric; 2 Wärtsilä Vasa 32E DG, 17,000 hp (12.5 MW); 2 Wärtsilä Vasa 32LNE DG, 4,216 hp (3.1 MW); 2 motors; 2 shafts; 1 bow thruster **Speed** 18 knots **Armament:** 2 x CIWS, 2 x 20mm guns (single) **Complement:** 325 Military Lift 303 troops, with an overload capacity of a further 405

Notes: These versatile vessels are designed to put Royal Marines ashore by air and by sea. ALBION has deck capacity for up to six Challenger 2 tanks or around 30 armoured all-terrain tracked vehicles. Floodable well dock able to take four utility landing craft. Four smaller landing craft carried on davits. Two-spot flight deck able to take medium support helicopters and stow a third. The flight deck allows the simultaneous operation of two Chinook helicopters. In 2017 ALBION, which had been laid up since 2012, completed a two-year £90m refit which will allow her to serve well into the 2030s. Part of the refit was a new cooling system to better operate in warmer climates, improved radar, new command system and the installation of Phalanx automated Gatling guns, replacing the old Goalkeeper system. She replaces BULWARK which entered a period of Extended Readiness (ER) in December 2016 until her upkeep in 2021. After the de-ammunitioning phase BULWARK will stay in Devonport until she emerges from refit in 2023. In October 2018 ALBION arrived in Oman to lead the naval element of the largest military exercise for UK forces since 2002. Exercise Saif Sareea (Swift Sword) saw more than 4,000 British personnel taking part alongside their Omani comrades in temperatures nudging 40°C.

HMS Dragon

DESTROYERS
DARING CLASS (Type 45)

Ship	Pennant Number	Completion Date	Builder
DARING	D32	2008	BVT Surface Fleet
DAUNTLESS	D33	2008	BVT Surface Fleet
DIAMOND	D34	2009	BVT Surface Fleet
DRAGON	D35	2011	BVT Surface Fleet
DEFENDER	D36	2012	BVT Surface Fleet
DUNCAN	D37	2013	BVT Surface Fleet

Displacement: 7,350 tonnes **Dimensions:** 152.4m x 21.2m x 5.7m **Machinery:** Integrated Electric Propulsion; 2 RR WR-21 GT alternators, 67,600 hp (49.7 MW); 2 Wärtsilä DG (4 MW); 2 Converteam motors (40 MW); 2 shafts **Speed:** 29 knots **Armament:** 1 - 4.5-inch gun, 2 x Quad Harpoon missile launchers (on four ships), Sea Viper missile system comprising Sylver VLS with combination of up to 48 Aster 15 and Aster 30 missiles, 2 x Vulcan Phalanx (fitted as required) **Aircraft:** Wildcat or Merlin **Complement:** 190 (with space for 235)

Notes: The Type 45 destroyers replaced the Type 42 destroyers, which were in service since 1978. Originally the requirement was for 12 vessels of the class, but the UK Ministry of Defence announced in July 2004 this would be cut to eight. This was further reduced in June 2008 to six previously contracted. All the destroyers entered into service by 2013 and their mission is to shield the Fleet from air attack using Sea Viper missiles which can knock targets out of the sky up to 70 miles away. DARING, the first Type 45, has had a very busy life since her commissioning in 2009 and one of her successes was her circumnavigation of the globe from May 2013 to February 2014. In July 2017 DARING became a harbour training ship in Portsmouth, where she will remain for two years until she starts her refit, replacing DAUNTLESS, which entered refit and subsequently rejoined the active fleet. DAUNTLESS was the second of the Type 45 and the first of the Daring Class destroyers to fire the new Sea Viper missile.

The first of the batch two destroyers - DRAGON - had her systems onboard upgraded in line with technological developments. She is also the fourth of the Royal Navy's six Type 45 air defence destroyers. DRAGON was launched on 7 November 2008 and after successful firing of the Sea Viper she was deployed on 19 March 2013 to the Gulf region. More recently DRAGON has been deployed for maritime security operations on the notorious drug smuggling route known as the 'Hash Highway' in the Gulf.

The ships are capable of contributing to worldwide maritime and joint operations in multi threat environments and are primarily air defence ships. The Sea Viper missile ensures that the ships can destroy incoming threats from the air whilst the Sampson Multi-Function Radar can simultaneously detect and track over four hundred targets, providing a fully automatic operation where rapid reaction is required.

Type 45 has an issue with the engine (Rolls Royce WR-21) and this is the 'intercooler-recuperator'. This should in theory recover heat, making the engine more efficient and crucially, reducing the ship's thermal signature. Unfortunately, it doesn't work properly and when it fails, the diesel generators can 'trip out', leaving the ship with no electrical power or propulsion. In 2014 a programme to improve the resilience of the Integrated Electric Propulsion system (IEP), co-funded by BAE Systems and the MoD, was set up (Project Napier) and concluded at the end of March 2015. The objective was to provide sufficient additional electrical generation capacity such that the IEP system can make cruise speeds (covering the major part of the Type 45 operating profile) on diesel alone. The project had two core work strands - the Equipment Improvement Plan (EIP) to enhance system reliability and to meet the original design intent in the near term while the longer term Power Improvement Plan (PIP) was intended to improve overall system resilience by adding upgraded diesel generators to provide the electrical generation capacity required to meet the overwhelming majority of propulsion and ship power requirements without reliance on the WR-21.

In March 2018 the MoD awarded a £160 million contract to BAE Systems, in collaboration with BMT Defence services and Cammell Laird for the Power Improvement Project (PIP). Two existing generators will be replaced with three larger units capable of delivering the ships propulsion and which will enhance the resilience of the Type 45 Class, The physical conversion work will be conducted at Cammell Laird's ship yard in Birkenhead, Merseyside. The first of class conversion is expected to complete in 2021, with follow on ships completed during the early 2020s.

HMS Northumberland

FRIGATES
TYPE 23 (ASW Variant)

Ship	Pennant Number	Completion Date	Builder
KENT	F78	2000	Yarrow
PORTLAND	F79	2000	Yarrow
SUTHERLAND	F81	1997	Yarrow
SOMERSET	F82	1996	Yarrow
ST ALBANS	F83	2001	Yarrow
WESTMINSTER	F237	1993	Swan Hunter
NORTHUMBERLAND	F238	1994	Swan Hunter
RICHMOND	F239	1994	Swan Hunter

Displacement: 4,900 tonnes **Dimensions:** 133m x 16.1m x 5.5m **Machinery:** CODLAG; 2 RR Spey GT, 31,100 hp (23.2 MW); 4 Paxman diesels 8,100 hp (6 MW); 2 GEC motors, 4,000 hp (3 MW); 2 shafts **Speed:** 28 knots **Armament:** Harpoon or Sea Ceptor; 1 x 4.5-inch gun, 2 x single 30mm guns, 4 x magazine launched Torpedo Tubes **Aircraft:** Wildcat or Merlin helicopter **Complement:** 185

Notes: The Type 23, or Duke Class, frigates are the core of the front-line Fleet and while primarily designed for anti-submarine warfare, they have evolved to operate in a general purpose role which today includes standing deployments with NATO formations, maritime counter-terrorism duties and humanitarian support. Today, the Duke Class remains at the forefront of the fleet's operations with (GP Variant) ARGYLL and MONTROSE currently deployed in the Far East.

The first Type 23 warships entered service in the 1990s and delivered a revolution in design and capability which continues to serve the fleet. Now, as the Royal Navy prepares for a new phase in its history with the arrival of the Queen Elizabeth carriers, the Type 23 force will provide escort and ride 'shotgun' alongside the new warships. Their task will be to keep ships away from the carrier, monitor the area for submarines and be ready to counter a suicide attack by small boat or a missile strike from a drone. In future, at least two Type 23s will join the carrier group on deployments operating alongside a Type 45 destroyer and nuclear attack submarine.

To make sure they are ready for this role (and capable of serving another 10-15 years) all are being overhauled to upgrade the entire 13-strong Type 23 fleet. The 8 x ASW variants incorporate 'Stealth' technology to minimise magnetic, radar, acoustic and infra-red signatures and are fitted with Type 2087 Sonar.

The £35 million per ship Life Extension (LIFEX) overhaul includes replacing the current weapons' systems with Sea Ceptor - a missile which can strike multiple targets and used to protect the carrier - although not all 13 Dukes will get the system. A new Artisan radar is to be installed and the warships will receive a Power Generation Machinery Upgrade (PGMU) engine upgrade, which involves replacement of the four main propulsion diesel-generator sets. The work programme started several years ago with the frigates being phased through the upgrade at Devonport. On average the upgrade takes 18-24 months with the last refit scheduled to complete by 2021. Some Type 23s who underwent an early refit but did not get the full machinery upgrade will need to go back into Devonport for engine overhaul. LIFEX will provide the frigates with a further decade or more of operational service, as the Royal Navy awaits the arrival of the Type 26.

The ships currently in refit include RICHMOND, which is due to be back in the fleet in late 2019. PORTLAND is also due back in the frontline later this year. SOMERSET is currently at Devonport awaiting refit and is due back in the fleet around 2020. ST. ALBANS, currently on exercise with an Astute-class submarine off western Scotland, is part of the active fleet and is due to start her refit later this year. WESTMINSTER was in Portsmouth at the start of the year. She is already fitted with Sea Ceptor, but has not yet received the engine upgrade. KENT has completed her refit and is awaiting her engine upgrade; she is currently at Plymouth undergoing Operational Sea Training. NORTHUMBERLAND is also active with the fleet and was deployed over the Christmas period. Meanwhile SUTHERLAND, a similar age to NORTHUMBERLAND, is in Devonport after a maintenance period, and while she has had a refit, she has not had the Sea Ceptor missile system fitted.

The planned decommissioning dates remain as: WESTMINSTER (2028); NORTHUMBERLAND (2029); RICHMOND (2030); SOMERSET (2031); SUTHERLAND (2032); KENT (2033); PORTLAND (2034) and ST. ALBANS (2035).

HMS Iron Duke

FRIGATES
TYPE 23 (GP Variant)

Ship	Pennant Number	Completion Date	Builder
LANCASTER	F229	1991	Yarrow
ARGYLL	F231	1991	Yarrow
IRON DUKE	F234	1992	Yarrow
MONMOUTH	F235	1993	Yarrow
MONTROSE	F236	1993	Yarrow

Displacement: 4,900 tonnes **Dimensions:** 133m x 16.1m x 5.5m **Machinery:** CODLAG; 2 RR Spey GT, 31,100 hp (23.2 MW); 4 Paxman diesels 8,100 hp (6 MW); 2 GEC motors, 4,000 hp (3 MW); 2 shafts **Speed:** 28 knots **Armament:** Harpoon or Sea Ceptor; 1 - 4.5-inch gun, 2 x single 30mm guns, 4 x magazine launched Torpedo Tubes **Aircraft:** Wildcat or Merlin helicopter **Complement:** 185

Notes: These five older Type 23s are not fitted with Type 2087 sonar and operate in the General Purpose role. They are scheduled to be replaced by the Type 31e frigate. LANCASTER, towed from Portsmouth to Plymouth to start her refit, is due back in the fleet in March 2019. Meanwhile, IRON DUKE, one of the older Dukes which has been sat in 'reduced readiness' at Portsmouth after her last major role escorting the QE during sea trials in 2017 was towed to Plymouth in 2018 for her refit. She clearly needs additional structure work after being allowed to decay at her moorings. MONMOUTH, MONTROSE and ARGYLL have all undergone their refits - although MONMOUTH is still to receive Sea Ceptor - and are all deployed on operations. The planned decommissioning dates remain as: ARGYLL (2023); LANCASTER (2024); IRON DUKE (2025); MONMOUTH (2026) and MONTROSE (2027).

HMS Hurworth

MINE COUNTERMEASURES SHIPS (MCMV)
HUNT CLASS

Ship	Pennant Number	Completion Date	Builder
LEDBURY	M30	1981	Vosper T
CATTISTOCK	M31	1982	Vosper T
BROCKLESBY	M33	1983	Vosper T
MIDDLETON	M34	1984	Yarrow
CHIDDINGFOLD	M37	1984	Vosper T
HURWORTH	M39	1985	Vosper T

Displacement: 750 tonnes FL **Dimensions:** 60m x 10.5m x 3.4m **Machinery:** 2 Caterpillar C32 ACERT diesels; 1 Deltic 9-55B diesel for pulse generator and auxiliary drive; 2 shafts; 1 bow thruster **Speed:** 15 knots **Armament:** 1 x 30mm; 2 x Miniguns **Complement:** 45 crew and 5 officers

Notes: The Hunt Class is a class of mine countermeasure vessels. As built, they combined the separate roles of the traditional minesweeper and that of the active minehunter in one hull. Later modifications saw the removal of mine-sweeping equipment. They have a secondary role as offshore patrol vessels.

In 2013 BAE Systems was awarded a six-year contract worth £15m to replace the propulsion systems on these ships, with the work to be carried out at Portsmouth. In 2016 BAE Systems and Finning Power Systems were more than halfway through the six-year project to refit eight Hunt Class minehunters with new systems. The refit will see the vessels receive new engines, gearboxes, bow thruster system, propellers, hydraulic systems and control and monitoring systems tailored to deal with the unique electromagnetic challenges posed by their role.

Each of the ships has been fitted with a set of twin Cat C32 ACERT engines (replacing the older Napier Deltics) coupled to twin-disc gearboxes. The new engine sets reduce the vessel's fuel demands significantly compared to the legacy engines they are replacing. Designed for minehunting and patrol missions, the Hunt Class represents the Royal Navy's biggest single-hulled warships to be made of glass-reinforced plastic (GRP). The GRP hull allows the ship to maintain a low magnetic signature, which is an essential part of keeping it safe from mines able to detect and target conventional metallic hulls. This means the engines being installed as part of the repower project need to be carefully designed to produce a very low electromagnetic field so they don't interfere with any electronic systems, whether they are on the ship or on those nearby.

Originally the Royal Navy commissioned 13 Hunt-class minesweepers and minehunters between 1980 and 1989. Two vessels, BICESTER (M36) and BERKELEY (M40) were transferred to the Greek Navy and renamed Europa and Callisto while BRECON (M29), COTTESMORE (M32) and DULVERTON (M35) had their mine countermeasures systems removed and were used as Northern Ireland Patrol Ships. The three vessels were decommissioned in September 2005 and BRECON was used as a training ship.

Eight remained in service with the Royal Navy. In December 2016 ATHERSTONE and QUORN were moved into the main ship hall at Portsmouth to undergo a mid-life overhaul where they were to receive new engines and sensors. However, in early 2017 the refits were cancelled and the two ships were quietly decommissioned and withdrawn from service on 14 December 2017.

In order to keep up the overseas deployment tempo, crews are swapped between ships. MIDDLETON and LEBDURY have been forward deployed to the Gulf since November 2015 and June 2017 respectively. The remaining vessels are all based at Portsmouth as the Second Mine Countermeasures Squadron (MCM2).

Published decommissioning dates are LEDBURY (2019), CATTISTOCK, BROCKLESBY, CHIDDINGFOLD and MIDDLETON (2020) and HURWORTH (2022). Although this is at odds with a press release from the RN on MIDDLETON's return to service back in 2014 following her refit and diesel replacement. It was stated that *"the new engines mean that MIDDLETON can sail faster, stay at sea longer, and will extend the ship's life to 2030 and beyond."* If this is the case it would appear that the Hunt Class will remain in service for quite some time with little hope of an immediate successor.

● CROWN COPYRIGHT/MOD   HMS Shoreham

SANDOWN CLASS

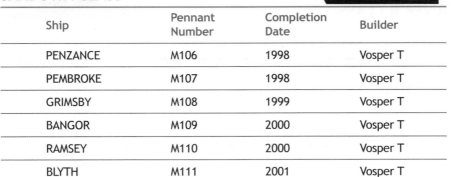

Ship	Pennant Number	Completion Date	Builder
PENZANCE	M106	1998	Vosper T
PEMBROKE	M107	1998	Vosper T
GRIMSBY	M108	1999	Vosper T
BANGOR	M109	2000	Vosper T
RAMSEY	M110	2000	Vosper T
BLYTH	M111	2001	Vosper T
SHOREHAM	M112	2001	Vosper T

Displacement: 600 tonnes **Dimensions:** 52.5m x 10.9m x 2.3m **Machinery:** 2 Paxman Valenta diesels, 1,523 hp; Voith-Schneider propulsion; 2 bow thrusters **Speed:** 13 knots **Armament:** 1 x 30mm gun; 2 x Miniguns; 3 x GPMG **Complement:** 34

Notes: The seven Sandown-class minehunters are all based at Faslane as the First Mine Countermeasures Squadron (MCM1). MCM1 can be found deployed on mine hunting in the Northern Gulf, busy in NATO exercises or clearing old ordnance that remains as a legacy of previous wars around the British coastline. MCM1 operates an eight crew rotation system where ships remains in the region for a number of years with crews being rotated roughly every six months. In September 2018 BANGOR returned back to base after her three year deployment in the Gulf. In May 2017 GRIMSBY received a full refit including a deep level maintenance, fit of new equipment upgrades (and a brand new sonar fit) and a new paint job.

HMS Forth

PATROL VESSELS
RIVER II CLASS

Ship	Pennant Number	Completion Date	Builder
FORTH	P222	2017	BAE Systems
MEDWAY	P223	2018	BAE Systems
TRENT	*P224*		*BAE Systems*
TAMAR	*P225*		*BAE Systems*
SPEY	*P226*		*BAE Systems*

Displacement: 2,000 tonnes **Dimensions:** 90.5m x 13.5m x 3.8m **Speed:** 24 knots **Armament:** 1 x 30mm; 2 x Miniguns, 2 x GPMG **Aviation:** Flight deck capable of receiving aircraft up to Merlin size **Complement:** 36 (accommodation for 70)

Notes: The new River II Class are based on the 90m vessels in service with Brazil and Thailand, but have been modified to meet specific RN requirements including a strengthened flight deck to accommodate a Merlin helicopter; modified and uprated helicopter in-flight refuelling arrangements, additional accommodation for embarked military detachments and improved watertight integrity and firefighting equipment. They feature BAE's CMS-1 combat management system, an I Band Doppler SharpEye radar for helicopter control and navigation and an E/F Band SharpEye radar for navigation and collision avoidance. The bridge is far more Type 45 (spacious, computerised with interchangeable displays, communications kit) than a rather cramped Type 23 frigate. FORTH was commissioned in April 2018. In March 2019 MEDWAY was handed over from BAE Systems and in July she will be heading for Portsmouth. The final ship SPEY began construction in April 2018 and is due to be delivered in 2019 and enter service by 2021.

HMS Mersey

PATROL VESSELS
RIVER CLASS

Ship	Pennant Number	Completion Date	Builder
TYNE	P281	2002	Vosper T
SEVERN	P282	2003	Vosper T
MERSEY	P283	2003	Vosper T

Displacement: 1,677 tonnes **Dimensions:** 79.5m x 13.6m x 3.8m **Machinery:** 2 MAN 12RK 270 diesels, 11,063 hp; 2 shafts; bow thruster **Speed:** 20+ knots **Armament:** 1 x 20mm; 2 x GPMG **Complement:** 48

Notes: Ordered on 8 May 2001, the deal was unusual in that the ships were leased from Vospers (VT) for five years under a £60 million contract. In January 2007 a £52 million lease-contract extension was awarded extending their RN service to the end of 2013. In September 2012 Whitehall signed a £39m contract to buy the ships outright, keeping them in service with the RN for the next ten years. The River class are now the only RN ships permanently conducting Fishery Protection patrols in the waters around England, Wales and Northern Ireland. Although this class could remain operational until 2022, it has been confirmed that they will be replaced by the River II Class vessels. Although SEVERN was decommissioned in October 2017 Defence Secretary Gavin Williamson announced in November 2018 that the future of the Batch 1 Offshore Patrols Vessels (OPVs), TYNE, MERSEY and SEVERN, was secured and that they would be retained for at least another two years.

31

HMS Clyde

RIVER CLASS OPV(H)

Ship	Pennant Number	Completion Date	Builder
CLYDE	P257	2006	VT Shipbuilding

Displacement: 1,847 tonnes **Dimensions:** 81.5m x 13.5m x 4.15m **Machinery:** 2 Ruston 12RK 270 diesels, 11,063 hp; 2 shafts; bow thruster **Speed:** 19 knots (full load) 21 knots (sprint) **Aircraft:** Flight deck to take Wildcat, Sea King or Merlin Helicopter **Armament:** 1 x 30mm gun; 5 x GPMG; 2 x Minigun **Complement:** 36 (space for additional 20 person-nel - see note)

Notes: Permanently deployed to the South Atlantic, CLYDE was designed to carry out patrol duties around the Falkland Islands and their dependencies. The ship is able to accommodate a single helicopter up to Merlin size. She is also able to embark a Military Force of up to 110 personnel (the size of the Roulement Infantry Company (RIC)) and move them around the Falkland Islands, inserting them at will. Like the previous River Class, she had been leased from BAE Systems, for a period of five years. In July 2011 it was announced that BAE Systems had been awarded a six-year contract extension to deliver support services to the ship until 2018. The annual cost to the public purse of operating the ship is £3.5 million. In October 2017 it was announced that HMS FORTH has been earmarked to replace CLYDE as permanent guardship of the Falklands with CLYDE slated for decommissioning at the end of 2019, at which time it will be sold to the Brazilian Navy.

HMS Scimitar

SCIMITAR CLASS

Ship	Pennant Number	Completion Date	Builder
SCIMITAR	P284	1988	Halmatic
SABRE	P285	1988	Halmatic

Displacemen:t 24 tonnes Dimensions: 16m x 4.7m x 1.4m Machinery: 2 MAN V10 diesels, 740 hp; 2 shafts Speed: 27+ knots Armament: 2 x GPMG Complement: 5 ratings and 1 officer

Notes: Assigned to the Royal Navy Gibraltar Squadron (RNGS) the vessels provide Force Protection to visiting warships, maritime security patrols within British Gibraltar Territorial Waters and support a variety of operations within the Joint Operating Area. In recent years the craft have been facing increasingly provocative stand-offs with their Spanish counterparts in the Guardia Civil as Spain tries to assert its influence over what it views as disputed waters in the Bay of Gibraltar. RNGS also operates three Rigid Hull Inflatable Boats (RHIBs). In July 2018 SCIMITAR made a rare visit away from Gibraltar which took her to the Algarve to exercise with the Portuguese Navy. After calling in at both Portimao and Vilamoura, SCIMITAR met up with Centauro-class patrol boat NRP PEGASO off Portimao to conduct a number of training exercises. PEGASO's main role is to conduct fishery protection duties around the Portuguese coast, extending as far as the Madeira archipelago. In September 2018 SABRE returned to the water following completion of her annual maintenance package. The Scimitar-class vessels were originally built for use on inland waterways in Northern Ireland and were first brought into service in 1993. Sabre was commissioned for the Royal Navy in 2003 and has served as part of the RNGS ever since.

HMS Puncher

COASTAL TRAINING CRAFT
P2000 CLASS

Ship	Pennant Number	Completion Date	Builder
EXPRESS	P163	1988	Vosper T
EXPLORER	P164	1985	Watercraft
EXAMPLE	P165	1985	Watercraft
EXPLOIT	P167	1988	Vosper T
ARCHER	P264	1985	Watercraft
BITER	P270	1985	Watercraft
SMITER	P272	1986	Watercraft
PURSUER	P273	1988	Vosper T
TRACKER	P274	1998	Ailsa Troon
RAIDER	P275	1998	Ailsa Troon
BLAZER	P279	1988	Vosper T
DASHER	P280	1988	Vosper T

Ship	Pennant Number	Completion Date	Builder
PUNCHER	P291	1988	Vosper T
CHARGER	P292	1988	Vosper T
RANGER	P293	1988	Vosper T
TRUMPETER	P294	1988	Vosper T

Displacement: 54 tonnes **Dimensions:** 20.8m x 5.8m x 1.8m **Machinery:** 2 Caterpillar C18 diesels, 1,746 hp; 2 MTU diesels, 2,000 hp (TRACKER); 2 shafts **Speed:** 20 knots **Armament:** 3 x GPMG (Faslane based vessels) **Complement:** 5 (with accommodation for up to 12).

Notes: Fourteen P2000 craft form the First Patrol Boat Squadron, whose primary role is to support the University Royal Naval Units (URNU) but also contribute to a wide range of Fleet tasking. Commodore Britannia Royal Naval College has overall responsibility for the URNUs whose role is to educate and inform a wide spectrum of high calibre undergraduates. Vessels are assigned to the following URNUs: ARCHER (East Scotland); BITER (Manchester & Salford); BLAZER (Southampton); CHARGER (Liverpool); DASHER (Bristol); EXAMPLE (Northumbria); EXPLOIT (Birmingham); EXPLORER (Yorkshire); EXPRESS (Wales); PUNCHER (London); PURSUER (Glasgow & Strathclyde); RANGER (Sussex); SMITER (Oxford); TRUMPETER (Cambridge).

The last two vessels built, RAIDER and TRACKER, comprise the Faslane Patrol Boat Squadron. They are fully-fledged armed patrol boats. Fitted with Kevlar armour and able to mount three 7.62mm General Purpose Machine Guns (GPMG), they are part of a growing Force Protection cadre based at Faslane to protect the UKs nuclear deterrent. These two vessels are fully engaged in FP duties and do not undertake university training.

In September 2018 fourteen P2000-class ships took part in their annual squadron exercise off the south coast of the UK. As well as providing training and maritime experience for the university students, the patrol vessels provide support to wider Fleet tasking and often take the role of attack craft in maritime exercise around the UK and Europe. Commanded by lieutenants with a small Royal Navy ship's company, university students also crew the ships to learn about the Service and to enjoy the camaraderie of working in a small team.

HMS Scott

SURVEY SHIPS
SCOTT CLASS

Ship	Pennant Number	Completion Date	Builder
SCOTT	H131	1997	Appledore

Displacement: 13,500 tonnes **Dimensions:** 131.5m x 21.5m x 8.3m **Machinery:** 2 Krupp MaK 9M32 diesels, 10,800 hp; 1 shaft, CP propeller; retractable bow thruster **Speed:** 17 knots **Complement:** 78

Notes:

Designed to commercial standards SCOTT provides the RN with a deep bathymetric capability off the continental shelf. Fitted with a modern multi-beam sonar suite she can conduct mapping of the ocean floor worldwide. She carries a mixture of the latest UK and US survey equipment. She operates a three watch system whereby the vessel is run by 42 of her ship's company of 78 - with the remainder on leave. Each crew member works 75 days on the ship before having 30 days ashore for leave, training and other duties, allowing her to spend more than 300 days at sea in a year. Her hull is Ice class 1A: ships with such structure, engine output and other properties are capable of navigating in difficult ice conditions, but only with the assistance of icebreakers. In 2013 Babcock won a five year contract from the MoD to provide through life engineering support to the ship. Rumours began to circulate that the vessel was to be withdrawn from service in 2018 as part of 'force adjustments' - however, a parliamentary written answer in October confirmed that, on current plans, her OSD is 2022.

HMS Enterprise

ECHO CLASS

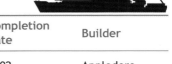

Ship	Pennant Number	Completion Date	Builder
ECHO	H87	2002	Appledore
ENTERPRISE	H88	2003	Appledore

Displacement: 3,500 tonnes **Dimensions:** 90.6m x 16.8m x 5.5.m **Machinery:** Diesel electric; 3 DG (4.8MW); 2 azimuth thrusters, 2,279 hp (1.7 MW); 1 bow thruster **Speed:** 15 knots **Armament:** 2 x 20mm **Complement:** 48 (with accommodation for 81)

Notes: In June 2000, a £130 million order was placed with prime contractor Vosper Thornycroft to build and maintain, over a 25 year period, these two new Survey Vessels Hydrographic Oceanographic (SVHO). Both vessels were built by sub-contractor Appledore Shipbuilding Ltd. They have a secondary role as mine countermeasures HQ ships. The total ship's company is 72, with 48 personnel onboard at any one time working a cycle of 75 days on, 30 days off, allowing the ships to be operationally available for 330 days a year. They are the first RN ships to be fitted with Azimuth pod thrusters in place of the more normal shaft and propeller. Each ship carries a named survey launch, SAPPHIRE (ECHO) and SPITFIRE (ENTERPRISE), equipped with side-scan sonar and both multi-beam and single-beam echo sounders.

In 2017 ENTERPRISE took over the role of flagship of NATO's Mine Counter-measures Group 2 while ECHO resumed her mission with the European Union Naval Force Mediterranean task group on Operation Sophia, preventing the illegal trafficking of people from Africa to Europe. In this role she saved the lives of more than 6,000 people, destroyed 65 dangerous rubber boats and skiffs, and handed over 15 suspected smugglers to European Naval Force authorities for potential prosecution.

In July 2018 ENTERPRISE returned home after a year-long NATO Flagship mission in the Mediterranean to an International Force of Minehunters. Having handed over to the German Navy, the Standing NATO Mine Countermeasures Group 2 (SNMCMG2) is one of four continuously deployed task groups which comprise NATO's Response Forces.

At the beginning of February 2019, while in the English Channel, ENTERPRISE passed close to the wreck of HMS GHURKA (as the name was spelled until the 1930s) and Commander Ladislaus decided to take a closer look at the WW1 torpedo boat as his hydrographers conducted a training wreck survey of the sunken warship.

GHURKA was assigned to the Dover Patrol, preventing U-boats slipping from the North Sea into the Channel and wider Atlantic. She hit a mine off Dungeness in a storm in February 1917 and sank rapidly, taking down all but five of her 79 crew.

Later that month ENTERPRISE 'scanned' the wreck of wartime submarine VANDAL, resting on the seabed off the Isle of Arran as she has done for the past 76 years. VANDAL was lost on trials in February 1943 – just four days after she was commissioned – entombing all 37 men aboard.

VANDAL's wreck was only discovered by minehunter HURWORTH 25 years ago, lying around 300ft down about a mile and a half off the northwestern tip of Arran. No cause of the disaster has been found.

HMS Magpie

INSHORE SURVEY VESSEL

Ship	Pennant Number	Completion Date	Builder
MAGPIE	H130	2018	Safehaven

Displacement: 37 tons **Dimensions:** 18m x 6.2m x 1.4m **Machinery:** 2 Volvo D16 diesels, 524 hp; 2 shafts **Speed:** 23 knots **Complement:** 12

Notes: In 2018 the small inshore survey craft GLEANER was replaced by MAGPIE, the largest of 38 new workboats being supplied to the MoD by Atlas Elektronik. The vessel is an 18 metre Wildcat 60 catamaran constructed by Safehaven Marine. It is capable of operating offshore for 7 days with 12 crew. Powered by twin Volvo D16 engines, the vessel has a 23kts maximum speed and a 1,400 nautical mile range at displacement survey speeds of 8-9kts.

According to Atlas Elektronik MAGPIE is a significant improvement over her predecessor, both in terms of equipment - she features better on-board equipment and have the capability of launching and recovering UUVs - and endurance.

Four small survey boats, NESBITT, PAT BARTON, COOK and OWEN are attached to the Hydrographic School at Devonport.

British Warships & Auxiliaries 2019

39

CROWN COPYRIGHT/MOD

HMS Protector

ICE PATROL SHIP
PROTECTOR

Ship	Pennant Number	Completion Date	Builder
PROTECTOR	A173	2001	Havyard Leirvik (Norway)

Displacement: 4,985 tonnes Dimensions: 89.7m x 18m x 7.25m Machinery: 2 Rolls Royce Bergen diesels, 9,602 hp; 1 shaft; CP propeller; bow and stern thrusters Speed: 15 knots Armament: Miniguns; GPMGs Complement: 88 (accommodation for up to 100)

Notes: The ice-breaker MV POLARBJØRN was initially leased, in June 2011, on a three-year contract from the Norwegian company GC Rieber Shipping as a temporary replacement for the damaged ENDURANCE and commissioned as PROTECTOR. In 2013 it was announced that the ship had been purchased by the MoD for £51 million.

Although the ship has a flight deck, there is no hangar, so she is unable to deploy with an embarked helicopter. However, for her latest deployment the ship has been given three 3D-printed micro-aircraft which are controlled from a laptop on board and can cruise at nearly 60 mph. Each one costs no more than £7,000 – cheaper than an hour's flying time by a FAA helicopter. Each micro-aircraft can fly for up to 30 minutes, recording video footage on a miniscule camera, before setting down in the icy waters or on the snow and ice where it will be picked up by PROTECTOR's ship's company.

She also operates the 10.5 metre ice-capable Survey Motor Boat JAMES CAIRD IV and the 8.5 metre Rigid Work Boat TERRA NOVA. She can also deploy two Pacific 22 RIBs (NIMROD and AURORA). She deploys with three BV206 all terrain vehicles and four quad bikes and trailers to assist in moving stores and equipment.

The ship sailed for her latest deployment in October 2015, but rather than operating in her more traditional waters of the South Atlantic, the ship headed east, visiting the Seychelles and Australia before embarking on survey operations in the Ross Sea, which has not been visited by a Royal Navy vessel for 80 years.

The ship has eight different 'work packages' planned in and around Antarctica. Those spells of intensive work, making use of the warmer temperatures and less inclement weather of the Austral summer, will focus on updating charts of the waters for the UK Hydrographic Office, monitoring wildlife and assisting the work of international inspectors who visit the numerous scientific bases peppered around the Antarctic. The ship was scheduled to be away from the UK until the spring of 2017, but in June 2017 it was revealed that she would not return until she had completed a third season in the Antarctic in 2018. One third of her crew rotates every few weeks to sustain the ship on operations.

In November 2017, following a request for assistance from the Argentine government, she was diverted to assist in the search for the missing Argentine submarine ARA SAN JUAN. A paragraph in the related press release further revealed that PROTECTOR is two years into a five-year deployment to the South Atlantic and Antarctica which would seem to indicate that she is not expected to return to the UK until 2020.

Summer 2018 saw PROTECTOR charting the waters around the remote British territory of Diego Garcia, the only island in the Chagos chain where there's human habitation. The island is a major UK/US military base and its waters had not been accurately surveyed for well over 180 years, prompting a ten-day concerted effort to rectify that fact. In September 2018 she returned to the frozen continent of Antarctica to chart poorly-mapped Antarctic waters, conduct environment studies and work alongside British and international scientists performing research into polar climate and wildlife. Afterwards she will retreat to South Africa to undergo maintenance and then head either up the West African coast or into the Indian Ocean, using her state-of-the-art suite of sensors to produce highly-accurate charts for use by seafarers the world over.

The Survey Motor Boat JAMES CAIRD IV (Daniel Ferro)

ROYAL MARINE CRAFT

RM Tamar, located within Devonport Naval Base, is home to the RMs Landing Craft, Hovercraft and other vessels when not required for deployment, either onboard the assault ships, or independently.

Based at RM Tamar is 1 Assault Group Royal Marines (1 AGRM), the lead for amphibious warfare and Royal Navy board and search training. The group is tasked with training and developing core amphibious and surface assault skills and equipment, including the provision of operational support for the Ministry of Defence.

1 AGRM is responsible for 4 subordinate units which deliver the vast spectrum of training and operations required in delivering amphibious and surface assault capability of the Royal Navy and Royal Marines.

10 (Landing Craft) Training Squadron - Responsible for delivering landing craftsmen training as well as small boats, engineering and assault navigation training.

11 Amphibious Trials and Training Squadron (Instow, North Devon) - Delivering training that covers the area between the craft and the beachhead. The Instow squadron also conducts the trials and testing of future craft.

The Royal Navy School of Board and Search at HMS RALEIGH in Torpoint trains both individuals and ships' boarding teams to conduct the full range of boarding operations that is required by the Naval Service.

In addition, 1 AGRM is also tasked with parenting the Assault Squadrons of the Royal Marines (ASRMs) and their Landing Craft detachments which are assigned to the amphibious assault ships. These ASRMs provide the landing craft and therefore the fighting capability for the RN's Amphibious Ships - ALBION and BULWARK.

43 Commando Fleet Protection Group Royal Marines (43 Cdo FP Gp RM) is based at HM Naval Base Clyde near Helensburgh on the West Coast of Scotland. Formerly Comacchio Group it was renamed in April 2012 and, together with 539 ASRM, became part of 3 Commando Brigade. The Group's core task is to provide military support to undertake final denial of access to nuclear weapons in addition to supporting the multi-agency force that protects nuclear weapons convoys. Additionally, specially trained teams are deployed at short notice to conduct tasks in support of the RN worldwide. Tasks have ranged from Force Protection, to conducting non-compliant boarding operations and counter-piracy operations.

Mull

ISLAND CLASS PATROL VESSELS

Ship	Pennant Number	Launch Date	Builder
RONA	-	2009	Holyhead Marine
MULL	-	2010	Holyhead Marine
EORSA	-	2014	Holyhead Marine

Displacement: 19.9 tonnes **Dimensions:** 14.9m x 4.6m x 0.9m **Machinery:** 2 Caterpillar diesels, 715 hp; 2 waterjets **Speed:** 33 knots **Armament:** 4 x GPMG **Complement:** 3

Notes: RONA and MULL were former Ministry of Defence Police vessels. They were fitted with three new weapons mounts, extra protection and communications equipment and transferred to 43 Commando Fleet Protection Group Royal Marines for operation on the Clyde to escort high value units such as the Vanguard-class submarines. A third vessel, EORSA, was delivered direct from the builders.

Landing Craft Utility (LCU)

LCU Mk10

Ship	Pennant Number	Parent Unit	Builder
9730	1001	1 AGRM	Ailsa, Troon
9731	1002	1 AGRM	Ailsa, Troon
9732	1003	HMS BULWARK	BAE Systems
9733	1004	HMS BULWARK	BAE Systems
9734	1005	HMS BULWARK	BAE Systems
9735	1006	HMS BULWARK	BAE Systems
9736	1007	1 AGRM	BAE Systems
9737	1008	1 AGRM	BAE Systems
9738	1009	1 AGRM	BAE Systems
9739	1010	1 AGRM	BAE Systems

Displacement: 240 tonnes **Dimensions:** 29.82m x 7.7m x 1.70m **Machinery:** 2 MAN Diesels; 2 Schottel propulsors; 1 bow thruster **Speed:** 10 knots **Armament:** 2 x GPMG **Complement:** 7

Notes: LCU Mk10 (Landing Craft Utility) are Ro-Ro style landing craft designed to operate from the Albion-class LPDs or Landing Ship Dock Auxiliary (LSDA). They have a 'drive-through' configuration, with ramps fore and aft and pilot house shifted to starboard. Ordered in 1998 from Ailsa Troon, the first two were delivered in 1999 with the final vessels being accepted into service in 2003. The remainder were built by BAE Systems at Govan. Capable of transporting one main battle tank or four large vehicles. Capacity for 120 fully equipped troops. With a range of around 600 nautical miles – more if auxiliary tanks are added – they are designed to operate independently for 14 days with a seven man Royal Marine crew in both arctic and tropical climates. All the crew members have bunk accommodation and there is a galley and store rooms.

CROWN COPYRIGHT/MOD

Landing Craft Vehicle and Personnel (LCVP)

Landing Craft Vehicle and Personnel (LCVP)

LCVP Mk5B

Ship	Pennant Number	Parent Unit	Builder
0202	B5	HMS BULWARK	Babcock Marine
0203	NM	HMS ALBION	Babcock Marine
0204	B6	HMS BULWARK	Babcock Marine
0205	P7	1 AGRM	Babcock Marine
0338	T6	1 AGRM	Babcock Marine
0339		HMS ALBION	Babcock Marine
0340	N2	HMS ALBION	Babcock Marine
0341	P9	1 AGRM	Babcock Marine
0344		1 AGRM	Babcock Marine
0345		1 AGRM	Babcock Marine
0346	N3	HMS ALBION	Babcock Marine
0347		HMS BULWARK	Babcock Marine
0353		HMS BULWARK	Babcock Marine

Ship	Pennant Number	Parent Unit	Builder
0354		1 AGRM	Babcock Marine
0355		1 AGRM	Babcock Marine
0356	B8	1 AGRM	Babcock Marine

Displacement: 24 tonnes Dimensions: 15.70m x 4.2m x 0.90m Machinery: 2 Volvo Penta diesels; 2 waterjets Speed: 25 knots Armament: 2 x GPMG Complement: 3

Notes: Designed to carry personnel and small vehicles, the first LCVP Mk5 (Landing Craft Vehicle and Personnel) was ordered in 1995 from Vosper Thornycroft and handed over in 1996. A further four were delivered in December 1996 with two more for training at RM Poole ordered in 1998. A further 16 were ordered from Babcock in 2001 with the final vessels being accepted into service in 2004. The Mk 5 can transport 8 tonnes of stores or a mix of 2 tonnes and 35 troops and operate from both ALBION and BULWARK. These vessels have a greater range, lift and speed than the Mk4s which they replaced. They feature aluminium hulls and are powered by twin waterjets. Their design includes a rigid and enclosed windowed canopy and a ramp at the bow that lowers for rapid unloading. GPMGs can be mounted when needed. The primary role is the landing of vehicles, personnel and equipment onto potentially hostile shores. The secondary role is a general purpose support craft both between ships and ship to shore. The craft are capable of performing normal duties in conditions up to sea state 4 and run for cover up to sea state 5. Pennant numbers and parent units can change as the vessels are rotated through maintenance cycles.

Landing Craft Vehicle and Personnel (LCVP)

Landing Craft Air Cushion (LCAC)

GRIFFON 2400TD LCAC

Ship	Pennant Number	Completion Date	Builder
C21	-	2010	Griffon
C22	-	2010	Griffon
C23	-	2010	Griffon
C24	-	2010	Griffon

G.R.T. 6.8 tons Dimensions: 13.4m x 6.8m Machinery: 1 Deutz diesel, 585 hp Speed: 45 knots Range: 300 nm Armament: 1 x GPMG Complement: 2 Crew; 16 fully-equipped marines.

Notes: Officially known as the Landing Craft Air Cushion (Light), the so-called 'floating fortress can carry 16 marines and race across water, ice and mud. Operated by 539 Assault Squadron, the 2400TD offers greater payload, performance and obstacle clearance than the earlier 2000 TD craft. Centre sections of the cabin roof can be removed in order to embark two 1 tonnes NATO pallets. Similiar to the 2000TD, the 2400TD's design allows the user to reduce the width of the craft with foldable side decks allowing it to be transported on a standard low loader truck or in the hold of a C-130 Hercules aircraft. They can also operate directly from the well-deck of RN amphibious ships. They are equipped with a 7.62mm General Purpose Machine Gun, HF and VHF radios, radar, GPS, ballistic protection and a variety of specialised equipment. All four entered service by the end of 2010.

CROWN COPYRIGHT/MOD   **Offshore Raiding Craftt**

OFFSHORE RAIDING CRAFT

Weight: 3.6 tonnes   **Dimensions:** 9.1m x 2.9m x 0.66m   **Machinery:** Twin Steyr MO256K43 250 bhp @ 4200rpm **Propulsion:** Rolls Royce FF270 Waterjets **Speed:** 36 knots   **Armament:** 1x HMG/GPMG forward, 2 x GPMG/HMG/GMG/Minigun aft **Complement:** 2 and 8 troops

Notes: The Royal Marines operate two versions of the Offshore Raiding Craft (ORC), the Troop Carrying Variant (TCV) and Fire Support Variant (FSV). The ORC is an air portable surface manoeuvre craft designed for the rapid deployment of 8 fully equipped troops and 2 crew from over the horizon (30 miles) ship-to-shore and vice versa. They provide rapid movement of troops in coastal, estuarine, riverine and inland waters. She has an aluminium hull with a low draught to allow for safe, rapid beach insertions. To provide ballistic protection for her 2 crew and passengers optional armour panels can be fitted.She can be transported as under-slung load by Chinook and Merlin helicopters or air-transported inside a C130 Hercules transport plane. Around 39 ORCs are in service with the Royal Marines. The ORC is manufactured by Holyhead Marine of Anglesey, North Wales.

RIGID RAIDING CRAFT

Notes: The Royal Marines operate a number of smaller Rigid-hulled and Rigid-Inflatable Craft for various assault, patrol and security duties. There are 5.2, 6.5 and 8 metre long versions. Rigid Raiders feature GRP (glass reinforced plastic) hulls and early varants featured single or twin outboard motors. A small team of men can carry the boats, even with engines attached, due to their lightweight construction. They can also be air-dropped out to sea. The latest RRC, the Mk3, is powered by a 240 hp inboard diesel engine but the Royal Marines might start replacing these with ORCs. They can carry up to eight troops. Rigid Raiders are manufactured by RTK Marine (part of the VT group).

Fast Insertion Craft

SPECIALIST CRAFT

In addition to the familiar Rigid Raiding Craft and Rigid Inflatable Boats other specialist vessels are available including the Fast Interceptor Craft (FIC) with a top speed of 60 knots. Back in July 2007 it was revealed that the Special Boat Service (SBS) were to take delivery of the so-called 'stealth boat'. The vessel is manufactured by Portsmouth-based VT Halmatic, which is now part of BAE Systems, but not much has been revealed about the vessel. The vessel has been spotted numerous times in waters off Poole, home of the SBS, and according to the BAE Systems Maritime web-site they are currently in service with UK Special Forces.

To maintain a low radar cross-section external fittings such as raydomes, aerial fits and apertures, on the craft are kept to a minimum. This results in low radar and heat signatures enabling a stealth capability. The specification of the boats in service with the UK Special Forces remain a mystery as there are numerous options not only for the propulsion lines (such as twin or triple petrol outboards through to twin diesel stern drives, twin diesel jet drives or twin Arneson surface drives) but also for the system facilities. Options include multiple fuel tank arrangements, water separa-tor/primary filter within the engine compartment, electric and manual bilge systems with automatic sensing and high bilge alarms, fire and/or smoke detection system with visual/audible display on console and/or cabin, variety of navigation and com-munication systems available to end user specification, including, but not limited to, fully integrated intercom systems, radar, satcom and multiple radio installation.

All craft are air transportable with special trailers available to suit different aircraft including A400M, C130 and C17.

Three models are available 33, 40 and 180.
Dimensions - Model 30: 10.75m x 2.59m x 0.7m
Dimensions - Model 40: 13.07m x 2.83m x 0.82m
Dimensions - Model 180: 18.1m x 3.8m x 0.9m

CB90 Combat Boats

SPECIALIST CRAFT

Following trials with Swedish CB90 Combat Boats, the Royal Marines were hopeful of procuring a new Force Protection Craft, based on experience with the CB90s, capable of landing troops and protecting the landing craft from seaborne and land based threats. An in service date of 2016 was anticipated but to date there has been little indication of progress with this programme. Specification - Weight: 18 tonnes Dimensions: 14.9m x 3.85m x 4.5m Power output: 2 x 600 kW Speed: 45 knots

Swimmer Delivery Vehicles (SDV), in reality miniature submarines, which can be deployed from dry deck shelters on larger submarines, are also operated as a part of the UK Special Forces inventory.

Swimmer Delivery Vehicle

SHIPS FOR THE FUTURE FLEET

TYPE 26 FRIGATE (City Class)

On 19 June 2017 the MoD awarded a £3.7 billion contract to BAE Systems for the construction of the first three Type 26 frigates, to be known as the City Class. The three frigates were named GLASGOW, CARDIFF and BELFAST. Manufacture of GLASGOW, the first of a planned class of eight ships, began on 20 July 2017 with a steel cutting ceremony at BAE Systems Naval Ships' facility at Govan on the Clyde.

Type 26 production is planned to extend into the mid-2030s with a contract for the second batch of five ships expected to be negotiated in the early 2020s. Production will run at an approximate 24-month drumbeat, with manufacture on CARDIFF to start in 2019 and BELFAST in 2021 with GLASGOW expected to enter service in 2026.

Designed for a service life of at least 25 years, they will form the backbone of the future RN surface fleet into the 2060s. Intended to replace eight anti-submarine warfare (ASW)-configured Type 23 frigates, the Type 26 has been conceived as an acoustically quiet surface combatant optimised for ASW but also capable of contributing to a wide range of other missions.

Key features of the design include a flexible mission bay amidships able to accommodate boats, mission payloads or stores; a 24-cell strike length Mk 41 vertical launcher; a Maritime Indirect Fire Support (MIFS) system based on the Mk 45 Mod 4 5-inch gun; the Sea Ceptor local area defence system (48 missiles accommodated in four eight-cell launchers); aviation facilities designed for the operation and support of two Wildcat helicopters or a single Merlin; a flight deck large enough to receive a Chinook ramp down and a secondary hangar space sized for a maritime unmanned air system.

The Type 26 platform comprises a 6,900 tonnes displacement steel monohull with a length of 149.9m, a beam of 20.8m, and a draught of 7.2m. A Combined Diesel Electric or Gas (CODLOG) machinery arrangement has been adopted combining a diesel-electrical system (four MTU 20V 4000 high-speed diesel generators and two shaft-mounted electric motors) for cruise speeds up to 18 knots, and a single direct-drive Rolls-Royce MT30 gas turbine, clutching in through a cross-connect gearbox, for a threshold sprint speed exceeding 26 knots. Range is put over 7,000 nm in Electric-Motor (EM) drive at 15 knots.

The Type 26 will be operated by a core crew of 157. Accommodation on board will provide for up to 208 personnel.

The MoD has confirmed that the £3.7 billion figure includes the procurement of new combat system equipment ship sets for the three Batch 1 ships. These include the Artisan Type 997 E/F-band 3D medium-range radar, the Sonar 2150 hull-mounted medium-frequency sonar, and the Sonar 2087 low-frequency active/passive variable depth system (the arrays will be supplied by MoD as Government Funded Equipment [GFE] from their existing sensor pool).

However, it does not include the cost of the Sea Ceptor system, which was ordered from MBDA in 2018 under a separate contract, or the Phalanx Block 1B close-in weapon system (which will be supplied as GFE from existing inventory).

In September 2018 it was announced that the first of the planned five Batch 2 ships would be BIRMINGHAM. And in November 2018, subsequent Batch 2 ships were announced as SHEFFIELD, NEWCASTLE, EDINBURGH and LONDON. Of the eight names, six were previously used as names of Type 42 destroyers, while the previous HMS LONDON was a Type 22 frigate.

To avoid future confusion with the BELFAST name the Imperial War Museum, that owns and operates the Second World War era light cruiser HMS BELFAST (C35), will rename her as 'HMS BELFAST (1938)".

● BABCOCK

GENERAL PURPOSE FRIGATE (TYPE 31e)

The Type 31e competitive design phase of the fast-tracked £1.25 billion programme to build an initial batch of five ships - in which BAE Systems/Cammell Laird and Babcock/BMT/Thales were the only contestants - was halted in July 2018. An article in The Times explained that the government competition for the Type 31 was suspended amid a funding crisis and sources warned that the Type 31 frigate may never materialise. Days later it was reported that the programme was to be restarted due to 'insufficient compliant bids' and the Ministry of Defence insisted the programme 'has not been cancelled'. On 10 December 2018, three groups were selected for the competitive design phase including BAE Systems/Cammell Laird with their planned Leander design - an evolution of BAE Systems' earlier Cutlass general purpose frigate concept (a stretched and modified development of the Khareef corvette design built for the Royal Navy of Oman); Babcock/BMT/Thales (known as Team 31) with their Arrowhead 140 design - a 'best of breed' based on Babcock's Arrowhead 120 design (pictured above) and builds on the pedigree of the 90m offshore patrol vessels built for the Irish Naval Service with elements of BMT's Venator-110 concept; and new comer Atlas Elektronik UK/Thyssenkrup Marine Systems, which is likely to be based on the MEKO A-200 design (currently in use with the Algerian and South African Navies).

Outline requirements for the Type 31e frigate include a hangar and flight deck big for a helicopter and unmanned air vehicles, sufficient accommodation to support the standard ship's company with mission specialists as required, and stowage for sea boats, disaster relief stores and other equipment. It will be operated by a crew of between 80-100, and is required to be sufficiently flexible to incorporate future developments in technology, including unmanned systems and directed energy weapons.

The plan is to award contracts by December 2019.

MILITARY AFLOAT REACH AND SUSTAINABILITY (MARS)

The future re-equipment of the RFA rests with the MARS programme which initially envisioned the procurement of five fleet tankers; three joint sea-based logistics vessels; two fleet solid-support ships and a single fleet tanker.

Post Strategic Defence and Security Review (SDSR) 2010, the government stated that the requirement for the MARS programme was driven by the logistic support needs of the future RN. It now seems that MARS will deliver just seven vessels (four Tide Class and up to three solid-support ships). With the tanker programme nearing completion, the MoD is turning its attention towards the other MARS component in the shape of the Future Solid Support (FSS) programme. This second element of the modernisation of the RFA is intended to introduce replacements for RFAs FORT AUSTIN, FORT ROSALIE and FORT VICTORIA from the early 2020s.

SDSR 2015 announced the planned acquisition of three FSS ships to enter service from the mid-2020s. The ships are required to have a total cargo capacity of up to 7000m3 and travel at a sustained speed of 18 knots without resupply. The platform must be capable of delivering material whilst underway and making 12 knots through the water and transferring single loads of up to 5 tonnes. In advance of starting the FSS procurement the MoD already contracted Rolls-Royce to develop, test and prove a new generation Heavy Replenishment at Sea rig (HRAS) that allows transfers of up to 5 tonnes at a time. The land based demonstrator has completed successful trials and is now installed at HMS Raleigh as part of a new RAS training facility.

Like the Tide-class tankers, the FSS have been classified as non-warlike and as a result it is likely that the £1 billion acquisition programme will be opened up to international competition. The project began its initial assessment phase in back April 2016 and the formal issue of documentation inviting bids for the design and build contract was issued in December 2018. The contract for design and build is to be awarded in 2020.

DREADNOUGHT CLASS SUBMARINE PROGRAMME

The £31 billion programme (previously referred to as the Successor) envisages the delivery of four SSBNs to replace the RN's four existing Vanguard-class submarines from 2028 to maintain Continuous At-Sea Deterrence (CASD).

At the end of March 2016 the government put its case for retaining the deterrent and won the backing of Parliament. In October it was announced that construction work was to start on the new submarines with £1.3 billion of new investment to move the programme to the Delivery phase with manufacturing work beginning on structural steel for the first submarine. At 152.9m (501ft) long, the new boats will be three metres longer than their predecessors and displace 1,300 tonnes more.

Construction on DREADNOUGHT, the lead ship in the class, started in October 2016.

Progress continues on the whole boat design, which is now 84% complete. Further design activities will mature during the build programme to ensure the most advanced systems and sub-systems are considered. The design includes separate quarters for female crew - a first for British submarines - and a new lighting system which can imitate night and day making it easier for crew to get used to normal life after three months submerged.

Over the last 12 months Rolls-Royce has made good progress on the submarine's PWR3 power plant, by developing new manufacturing processes and methods. As a result, the design and manufacture of the reactor remains on track for delivery to BAE Systems' shipyard at Barrow-in-Furness. BAE Systems are completing the integration of this new power plant into the overall submarine design. Early phase secondary propulsion steelwork has been manufactured in the New Assembly Shop at Barrow and the fabrication of all the major propulsion equipment has been delivered.

All components for the nuclear steam production system for the first Dreadnought submarine has now been delivered to Barrow.

The missile tubes for the Dreadnought Programme are part of the UK-US Common Missile Compartment project. The equipment necessary to weld the missile tubes has been procured from the US, and installation at Barrow commenced in April 2017. Approval was given in 2017 to extend the planned life of the Trident II D5 missile electronic packages. This decision led to an increased total project cost to around £350 million. These life extension programmes provide sufficient Trident II D5 missile packages, including spares, to support the UK's current stock entitlement.

The UK is also updating the Mark 4 warhead by introducing the new Mark 4A non-nuclear Arming, Fusing and Firing system to the warhead. This replacement is required as the older unit becomes obsolete.

In December 2018 the Defence Secretary Gavin Williamson announced that the second Dreadnought-class ballistic missile submarine will be named VALIANT. In addition to naming the submarine, Mr Williamson announced a £400 million funding boost for the Dreadnought programme. The latest investment comes after £960 million worth of contracts were announced in May 2018 to ramp up the current phase of construction for the four nuclear-armed Dreadnought submarines.

On 25 February 2019, the First Sea Lord announced that the third Dreadnought-class submarine will be named WARSPITE. The boat will take her place in the Fleet in the 2030s, alongside DREADNOUGHT, VALIANT and a fourth, as yet unnamed, submarine, each carrying Trident nuclear missiles on deterrence patrols for three months at a time.

In the January/February 2019 issue of *Warship World* it was revealed that in the current Financial Year 2018/19 the MoD will be spending £5.2 billion on the Defence Nuclear Enterprise (DNE), of which £1.8 billion will be on construction and support of submarines, £1.4 billion on missiles and warheads and £220 million on managing the overall programme. At the same time, the MoD needs to bridge a £3 billion affordability gap in its budget. This is in stark contrast to the 2017 update to parliament which indicated that the Dreadnought programme remained within its £31 billion budget, with £4.3 billion spent so far on the design and early manufacture phase (£900 million of which was spent in Financial Year 2016/17).

In 2009, the Commons Committee of Public Accounts reported that the the MoD needed to be bringing into service the new Dreadnought Class by 2024. However, the MoD now expects to introduce the new class from the early 2030s. This means that the Vanguards will have to remain operational for at least 37 years, 13 years longer than the design-life for the class.

HMS Defender

THE ROYAL FLEET AUXILIARY

The Royal Fleet Auxiliary (RFA) is a civilian manned fleet owned by the Ministry of Defence. Traditionally, its main task has been to replenish warships of the Royal Navy at sea with fuel, food, stores and ammunition to extend their operations away from base support. However, as the RN surface fleet has shrunk, the RFA has shrunk with it but it has also acted as a 'force multiplier' being able to take on some operational roles. By embarking helicopters, tankers and stores ships have been deployed on RN patrol tasks in the Caribbean, on counter-piracy operations in the Indian Ocean and, more recently, on operations in the eastern Mediterranean in support of the migrant crisis. By embarking ASW helicopters they are also able to provide additional warfare support to task group operations.

As part of the Military Afloat Reach and Sustainability (MARS) programme, the MoD placed an order in 2012 for four tankers to be built in South Korea,where they were built by Daewoo Shipbuilding & Marine Engineering. The first of class, TIDESPRING, entered service in 2017 whilst TIDERACE joined her in September 2018. At that time TIDESURGE completed her customisation programme and was about to embark on Capability Assessment Trials with the aim to be in service by the end of 2018.

In August 2018 the final of the four Tide-class tankers – TIDEFORCE – arrived in Cornwall where it would undergo military customisation and armament before starting sea trials. Customisation work, including the installation of communications equipment and defensive systems, will be performed by A&P Falmouth. Work on TIDEFORCE was expected to take several months with the ship then due to enter service in 2019.

With the arrival of the Tide-class tankers the long serving GOLD ROVER and BLACK ROVER, the last examples of the Rover Class, were decommissioned in 2017 and moved to Portsmouth to await disposal.

The long term maintenance of the RFA fleet rests with shipyards in the North West, North East and South West of England. Cammell Laird Shiprepairers & Shipbuilders Ltd of Birkenhead and the A&P Group in Falmouth and Newcastle-upon-Tyne were named as the contractors to maintain the flotilla of 13 RFA tankers, stores and landing ships. They maintain 'clusters' of ships, providing the necessary refuelling and refit work for the RFA vessels throughout their service lives. Ships are grouped in clusters according to their duties and capabilities. A&P Group are charged with two clusters (Cluster 1: ARGUS and Cluster 2: CARDIGAN BAY, LYME BAY, MOUNTS BAY) in a contract worth around £53 million with the work to be shared between its bases in Falmouth and on the Tyne. In 2016 A&P were awarded a contract to provide through-life support to all four Tide-class tankers in service for a minimum of three years. Cammell Laird is contracted for the maintenance of three clusters of ships (Cluster 4: WAVE KNIGHT, WAVE RULER; Cluster 5: FORT AUSTIN, FORT ROSALIE and Cluster 6: FORT VICTORIA).

SHIPS OF THE ROYAL FLEET AUXILIARY
Pennant Numbers

Ships	P. No.	Page	Ships	P. No.	Page
Tankers			Stores Ship/Tankers		
TIDESPRING	A136	62	FORT VICTORIA	A387	64
TIDERACE	A137	62			
TIDESURGE	A138	62	Amphibious Ships		
TIDEFORCE	A139	62			
WAVE KNIGHT	A389	61	LYME BAY	L3007	65
WAVE RULER	A390	61	MOUNTS BAY	L3008	65
			CARDIGAN BAY	L3009	65
Stores Ships					
			Primary Casualty Receiving		
FORT ROSALIE	A385	63	Ship/Aviation Training Ship		
FORT AUSTIN	A386	63			
			ARGUS	A135	67

RFA Tidespring

RFA Wave Knight

FAST FLEET TANKERS
WAVE CLASS

Ship	Pennant Number	Completion Date	Builder
WAVE KNIGHT	A389	2002	BAe Systems
WAVE RULER	A390	2002	BAe Systems

Displacement: 31,500 tonnes (FL) **Dimensions:** 196.5m x 28.25m x 10m **Machinery:** Diesel-electric: 4 Wärtsilä DG, 25,514 hp (18.76 MW); 2 GEC Alstom motors with variable speed converters, 19,040 hp (14 MW); 1 shaft; 1 bow and stern thruster **Speed:** 18 knots **Armament:** 2 x Vulcan Phalanx, 2 x 30mm **Aircraft:** Up to 2 Merlin **Complement:** 80 (plus 22 Fleet Air Arm)

Notes: These 31,500 tonnes ships are diesel-electric powered and have the capability to supply fuel and other liquid cargo to vessels using three replenishment rigs on port and starboard beams and through a Hudson reel-type stern rig. They have a cargo capacity of up to 16,900 tonnes for fuel and 915 tonnes of dry stores. The ships are also able to deliver fuel to dracones positioned alongside during amphibious operations. She can carry a full medical team and sick bay and are capable of distributing 2,000 emergency relief packages in times of crisis. In addition, reverse-osmosis equipment is fitted enabling the production of 100m3 of drinkable water per day. They have a large one spot flight deck, hangar and maintenance facilities capable of supporting two Merlin helicopters. A Royal Navy Wildcat or a United States Coast Guard helicopter is embarked during her Atlantic Patrol Task deployment. To prevent or reduce environmental pollution from oil spills if damage is sustained to the outer hull the vessels were designed with double hulls. In June 2018 it was reported by the Brazilian press that the MoD had offered to sell one or both of the Wave-class tankers to Brazil.

RFA Tidesurge

FLEET TANKERS
TIDE CLASS

Ship	Pennant Number	Completion Date	Builder
TIDESPRING	A136	2017	Daewoo Shipbuilding
TIDERACE	A137	2018	Daewoo Shipbuilding
TIDESURGE	A138	2018	Daewoo Shipbuilding
TIDEFORCE	A139	2019	Daewoo Shipbuilding

Displacement: 39,000 tonnes (FL) **Dimensions:** 200.9m x 28.6m x 10m **Machinery:** 2 Wärtsilä diesels, 20,394 hp; 2 shafts **Speed:** 26.8 knots **Armament:** 2 x Phalanx CIWS; 2 x 30mm **Aircraft:** 1 x Merlin or Wildcat **Complement:** 63 (plus 26 spare berths)

Notes: A derivative of BMT Defence Services' AEGIR-26 design, they are double-hulled to prevent oil being lost by damage to the outer hull. Replenishment facilities comprise three abeam RAS(L) stations (two sited starboard and one to port) for diesel oil, aviation fuel and fresh water; solid RAS reception up to 2 tonnes; and vertical replenishment using an embarked helicopter. Provision is also made for the future fit of a stern fuel delivery reel. In June 2018 QUEEN ELIZABETH successfully took on fuel 'on the go' from TIDESPRING for the first time in the North Atlantic. The aircraft carrier practised the replenishment-at-sea (RAS) to take on supplies on both her port and starboard sides. As the lines were passed and the fuel hose transferred to hook up with the intake on the carrier the two ships were just 42m apart sailing along at 12 knots. TIDESPRING can deliver 800 cubic metres of fuel an hour but on this occasion 220 cubic metres of F76 marine fuel was sent across as the RAS was more about testing the principle rather than the carrier's tanks running low.

RFA Fort Rosalie

STORES VESSELS
FORT CLASS I

Ship	Pennant Number	Completion Date	Builder
FORT ROSALIE	A385	1978	Scott Lithgow
FORT AUSTIN	A386	1979	Scott Lithgow

Displacement: 23,384 tonnes **Dimensions:** 183m x 24.1m x 9m **Machinery:** 1 Sulzer 8-cylinder RND90 diesel, 22,300 shp; 1 shaft; 2 bow thrusters **Armament:** 2 x Phalanx CIWS **Speed:** 22 knots **Complement:** 201, (120 RFA, 36 MoD Civilians & 45 Fleet Air Arm)

Notes: Designed to replenish all kinds of armaments and victualling stores while underway. Full hangar and maintenance facilities are provided and up to four Sea King or Wildcat helicopters can be carried on the 2 flight decks, one at the stern and one spot on top of the hanger, for both the transfer of stores and anti-submarine protection of a group of ships (Note: they are not cleared to operate Merlin). They can replenish-at-sea via 6 stations, three on each side as well as using helicopters for vertical replenishment. Both ships can be armed with 2 - 20mm Oerlikon/ BMARC KAA guns in GAM-B01 mounts and 4 × 7.62mm L7 GPMGs. The ships were ordered in 1971 and saw service in the Falklands War, the then FORT GRANGE (she was renamed to FORT ROSALIE in 2000 to avoid confusion with the new Fort Victoria-class replenishment oiler FORT GEORGE) being shadowed by Argentine Air Force C-130 Hercules aircraft while still 1,000 nautical miles from the combat area and FORT AUSTIN being attacked while sitting in San Carlos water. FORT AUSTIN also supported the British intervention in Sierra Leone in 2000 and was mothballed in 2009 but reactivated following the 2010 SDSR. Both had major refits at Cammell Laird to enable another decade of service. In 2011 it was announced that the service of FORT AUSTIN and FORT ROSALIE would be extended by another two years to 2023 and 2024 respectively. They will ultimately be replaced by the new Solid Support Ships.

CROWN COPYRIGHT/MOD

RFA Fort Victoria

REPLENISHMENT SHIPS
FORT CLASS II

Ship	Pennant Number	Completion Date	Builder
FORT VICTORIA	A387	1992	Harland & Wolff

Displacement: 33,675 tonnes **Dimensions:** 204m x 30m x 9m **Machinery:** 2 Crossley-Pielstick V-16 diesels, 23,904 hp; 2 shafts **Speed:** 20 knots **Armament:** 2 x 30mm Oerlikon / BMARC KAA guns in GAM-B01 mounts, 2 x Phalanx CIWS, 15 cell Sea Wolf Missile System (fitted for but not with) **Complement:** 95 RFA, 24 MoD Civilians, 15 RN and up to 154 Fleet Air Arm

Notes: A "One stop" replenishment ship with the widest range of armaments, fuel and spares carried. Can operate up to 5 Wildcat or 3 Merlin Helicopters (more in a ferry role) with full maintenance facilities onboard. Medical facilities were upgraded with a 12 bed surgical capability. Originally these ships were designed with the Sea Wolf vertical launch surface-to-air missile system to defend both themselves and the lightly armed Type 23 frigates during their North Atlantic anti-submarine role. The Type 23 emerged as a much more potent, multi-role vessel each carrying the Sea Wolf missile and there was no need for her to carry any missiles. Early 2018, the 24-year old FORT VICTORIA visited Cammell Laird for both an overhaul and modifications to meet the demands of global environmental regulators and to support the Royal Navy's new carriers. Both shipwrights and technicians fitted extra protective hulls to the fuel tanks – used to re-supply smaller vessels than the carriers (as two refuels of QUEEN ELIZABETH would effectively empty her tanks). In November 2018 she was heading for Faslane as her sailors prepared her for renewed duties in the QUEEN ELIZABETH's task group.

RFA Cardigan Bay

LANDING SHIP DOCK (AUXILIARY)
BAY CLASS

Ship	Pennant Number	Completion Date	Builder
LYME BAY	L3007	2007	Swan Hunter
MOUNTS BAY	L3008	2006	BAe Systems
CARDIGAN BAY	L3009	2007	BAe Systems

Displacement: 16,190 tonnes **Dimensions:** 176.6m x 26.4m x 5.8m **Machinery:** Diesel-electric; 2 Wärtsilä 8L26 DG, 6,000 hp (4.5 MW); 2 × Wärtsilä 12V26 DG, 9,000 hp (6.7 MW); 2 azimuthing thrusters; 1 bow thruster **Speed:** 18 knots **Armament:** 2 x Phalanx CIWS (exact weapons fit varies within the class) **Complement:** 60

Notes: The dock is capable of operating LCU 10s and they carry two LCVP Mk5s. They can offload at sea, over the horizon. In addition to their war fighting role they could be well suited to disaster relief and other humanitarian missions. Although the ships are fitted for a single serviced helicopter landing spot, two medium-size helicopters (Merlin) can be operated simultaneously. The helicopter deck structure is reinforced and can support operations by a Chinook helicopter or an MV-22 Osprey tiltrotor aircraft. In June 2018 CARDIGAN BAY participated in Mine Countermeasures Exercise 18-2 in the Gulf. The exercise is designed to see how the navies of Britain and the USA can combat the 21st-Century mine threat.In October 2018, after a 5,000-mile journey LYME BAY arrived in the new port of Duqm in Oman to participate in Exercise Saif Sareea. Britain has permanent facilities in Duqm to support her naval operations in the region. Early February 2019, US Marines invited the Protection Team from 42 Commando – currently attached to CARDIGAN BAY - to participate in FASTCENT and improve their board and search/protection skills.

HMS Duncan (front) and HMS Dragon

RFA Argus

PRIMARY CASUALTY RECEIVING SHIP/
AVIATION TRAINING SHIP

Ship	Pennant Number	Completion Date	Builder
ARGUS	A135	1981	Cantieri Navali Breda

Displacement: 28,481 tonnes (Full Load) **Dimensions:** 175.1m x 30.4m x 8.1m
Machinery: 2 Lindholmen Pielstick 18 PC2.5V diesels, 23,400 hp; 2 shafts; 1 bow thruster
Speed: 18 knots **Armament:** 4 x 30mm, 2 x 20mm **Aircraft:** up to 6 Merlin
Complement: 254 (inc 137 FAA)

Notes: The former Italian-built container ship MV CONTENDER BEZANT was purchased in 1984 and rebuilt from 1984-87 at Harland and Wolff, Belfast, to operate as an Aviation Training Ship. She undertook a rapid conversion in October 1990 to become a Primary Casualty Receiving Ship (PCRS) for service in the Gulf. These facilities were upgraded and made permanent during 2001. In 2009 the ship underwent a Service Life Extension Programme at Falmouth to switch her primary role to that of PCRS with a secondary aviation training role. The construction of new casualty access lifts together with a new deckhouse aft of the superstructure has reduced helicopter capability by one landing spot. The ship has facilities for undertaking 3 major operations simultaneously, intensive care, high dependency and general wards for up to 100 patients. It also has a dentistry operating theatre, CT scanner and X-ray units. The care facility operates with a staff of up to 250 doctors, nurses and support staff. As the ship is armed (2 × Oerlikon 20mm/85 KAA on GAM-BO1 mountings and 4 × 7.62mm GPMGs Mk44 Miniguns) and is not painted in the required white with red crosses, the Geneva Convention prevents her from being officially classified as a hospital ship. The ship is scheduled to remain in service until 2024 although, to date, there appears to be no planned replacement.

● DANIEL FERRO   **MT Maersk Raleigh**

COMMERCIAL TANKER

Ship	Completion Date	Builder
MAERSK RALEIGH	2005	Guangzhou Shipyard, China

Displacement 22,184 tonnes (GRT); 35,191 tonnes (DWT) **Dimensions** 172m x 28m x 8.3m **Machinery** 2SA 5 cylinder Burmeister & Wain diesel, 9,721 hp; 1 shaft; bow thruster **Speed** 14.5 knots

Notes: The MoD has the commercial tanker MAERSK RALEIGH under charter which supplies fuel to the naval facilities in the UK and abroad. The MoD charters the vessel to commercial companies when it is not in use for their own requirements. MAERSK RALEIGH is the ex ROSA MAERSK and was renamed and reflagged (to UK flag) in August 2017. She has taken over from MAERSK RAPIER which was sold in June 2017 to an unnamed party for USD6.5 million and renamed DOLICHA BAY. The tanker MT CUMBRIAN FISHER has also been occasionally chartered for moving fuel products between the UK and the Falkland Islands. The charter might come to an end as at the end of January 2019 Nautilus International - the Union for Maritime & Shipping Professionals at sea, ashore & inland waterways - announced that Maersk would be taking their remaining vessels off the UK Ship Register, exiting the UK Tonnage Tax and ending the training of UK cadets.

● DANIEL FERRO   **MV Eddystone**

STRATEGIC SEALIFT RO-RO VESSELS
POINT CLASS

Ship	Pennant Number	Completion Date	Builder
HURST POINT		2002	Flensburger
HARTLAND POINT		2002	Harland & Wolff
EDDYSTONE		2002	Flensburger
ANVIL POINT		2003	Harland & Wolff

Displacement: 10,000 tonnes, 13,300 tonnes (FL) **Dimensions:** 193m x 26m x 7.6m
Machinery: 2 MaK 94M43 diesels, 21,700 hp; 2 shafts; 2 CP propellers; 1 bow thruster
Speed: 18 knots **Complement:** 18-22

Notes: Foreland Shipping Limited operated 6 Ro-Ro vessels built at yards in the UK and Germany under a Private Finance Initiative (PFI) deal which was signed with the MoD on 27 June 2002 and runs until 31 December 2024. While the current main focus is on transporting equipment to and from the Middle East/Gulf in support of military activities, the vessels also make regular voyages to the Falkland Islands, Canada and Norway in support of training exercises. Each vessel can carry 130 armoured vehicles and 60 trucks and ammunition or 8,000 tonnes of vehicles. There is 2,650 linear metres of space for vehicles. It can transport up to four helicopters including Chinook, Apache, Merlin and Wildcat. The ships are all named after English lighthouses. They come under the operational umbrella of Defence Supply Chain Operation and Movements (DSCOM), part of the Defence Logistics Organisation. In 2012 the requirement was reduced from six to four ships. BEACHY HEAD and LONGSTONE were subsequently sold.

RFA ROSALIE being slipped to sail from C Buoy in Plymouth Sound supported by SD FORCEFUL, SD HERCULES and SD ASSIST (John Shore)

SERCO MARINE SERVICES

In December 2007 the MoD signed a £1 billion Private Finance Initiative (PFI) contract with Serco Denholm Marine Services Limited for the Future Provision of Marine Services (FPMS) over the following 15 years. In 2009 Serco bought out Denholm's share and the SD funnel logos were replaced by a prominent Serco logo on the superstructure.

Marine services embrace a wide range of waterborne and associated support activities, both in and out of port, at Portsmouth, Devonport and on the Clyde, as well as maintenance of UK and overseas moorings and navigational marks and support of a range of military operations and training.

In-port services include the provision of berthing and towage activities within the three naval bases; passenger transportation, including pilot transfers and the transportation of stores, including liquids and munitions. The recovery and disposal of waste from ships and spillage prevention and clean-up also fall within their tasking. There is also a requirement for substantial out-of-port operations. Diving training, minelaying exercises, torpedo recovery, boarding training and target towing duties are also undertaken.

The Briggs Group has been sub-contracted to assist with buoys and mooring support work. Shore based work to support these moorings and navigation buoys have been relocated from Pembroke Dock to Burntisland on the Firth of Forth.

SHIPS OF SERCO MARINE SERVICES

Ship	Page	Ship	Page
SD ADEPT	76	SD MOORFOWL	94
SD ANGELINE	96	SD MOORHEN	94
SD BOUNTIFUL	75	SD NAVIGATOR	95
SD BOVISAND	85	SD NETLEY	86
SD CAREFUL	76	SD NEWHAVEN	86
SD CATHERINE	80	SD NORTHERN RIVER	93
SD CAWSAND	85	SD NORTON	89
SD CHRISTINA	78	SD NUTBOURNE	86
SD CLYDE RACER	97	SD OBAN	88
SD CLYDE SPIRIT	98	SD OCEANSPRAY	92
SD DEBORAH	78	SD OILMAN	92
SD DEPENDABLE	75	SD OMAGH	88
SD EILEEN	78	SD ORONSAY	88
SD EMILY	*80*	SD PADSTOW	87
SD ENGINEER	95	SD POWERFUL	76
SD EVA	*90*	SD RAASAY	95
SD FAITHFUL	76	SD RELIABLE	75
SD FLORENCE	79	SD RESOURCEFUL	75
SD FORCEFUL	76	SD SOLENT RACER	97
SD FRANCES	*79*	SD SOLENT SPIRIT	98
SD GENEVIEVE	79	SD SUZANNE	78
SD HELEN	79	SD TAMAR RACER	97
SD HERCULES	77	SD TAMAR SPIRIT	98
SD IMPETUS	72	SD TEESDALE	92
SD IMPULSE	72	SD TEMPEST	73
SD INDEPENDENT	74	SD TILLY	81
SD INDULGENT	74	SD VICTORIA	82
SD INSPECTOR	95	SD WARDEN	83
SD JUPITER	77	SD WATERPRESS	92
SD KYLE OF LOCHALSH	84		
SD MARS	77	**Briggs Sub-Contract**	
SD MELTON	*91*		
SD MENAI	91	CAMERON	99
SD MEON	91	KINGDOM OF FIFE	99

Entries displayed in lighter typeface have been removed from contract and are awaiting sale.

    SD Impulse

TUGS

IMPULSE CLASS

Ship	Completion Date	Builder
SD IMPULSE	1993	Richard Dunston (Hull)
SD IMPETUS	1993	Richard Dunston (Hull)

G.R.T.: 319 tonnes **Dimensions:** 32.5m x 10.5m x 5.2m **Machinery:** 2 Allen 8S12 F-BC diesel engines; 3,400 hp; 2 Azimuth thrusters; 1 bow thruster **Speed:** 12 knots **Complement:** 5

Notes: Completed in 1993 specifically to serve as berthing tugs for the Trident-class submarines at Faslane. In February 2018 IMPULSE underwent a 25 year special survey in Garvel. Both her main engines underwent full overhaul as did both Aqua master propulsion units. Other work included the overhaul of the main forward and aft winches, all electrical and lifesaving equipment had annual checks and service and the ship's crane was serviced and load tested. Both are to be retained in service until 2022.

SD Tempest

ART 8032 CLASS

Ship	Completion Date	Builder
SD TEMPEST	2017	Damen (Poland)

G.R.T.: 495 tonnes **Dimensions:** 32.9m x 13.2m x 6.2m **Machinery:** 3 Caterpillar 3512C diesels, 5,295 kW; 3 Schottel SRP 1215 CP propellers **Speed:** 13 knots **Complement:** 4

Notes: Ordered in February 2016 her primary role in Portsmouth is to support the Queen Elizabeth Class carriers although she will undertake other harbour towage work when not required in her primary role. She was launched in Gdansk (Poland) on 14 September 2016 and arrived at Portsmouth in February 2017. With a bollard pull of 80 tonnes she is the most powerful tug in the fleet. Equipped with a double drum render/recovery aft winch. Fitted with a foldable mast to allow her to operate under the flightdeck overhangs. Bollard pull 82 tonnes.

SD Independent

ASD 2509 CLASS

Ship	Completion Date	Builder
SD INDEPENDENT	2009	Damen (Netherlands)
SD INDULGENT	2009	Damen (Netherlands)

G.R.T.: 345 tonnes approx   Dimensions: 25.14m x 9.44m x 4.45m   Machinery: 2 Caterpillar diesels; 3,500 hp; 2 RR thrusters; 1 bow thruster   Speed: 13 knots   Complement: 4

Notes: Azimuth Stern Drive (ASD) tugs. Designed for Coastal and Harbour towage, specifically modified for making cold moves within the Naval Bases. Both INDEPENDENT and INDULGENT are based at Portsmouth. Bollard pull 40 tonnes.

● LEE HARRISON

ATD 2909 CLASS

Ship	Completion Date	Builder
SD RELIABLE	2009	Damen (Netherlands)
SD BOUNTIFUL	2010	Damen (Netherlands)
SD RESOURCEFUL	2010	Damen (Netherlands)
SD DEPENDABLE	2010	Damen (Netherlands)

G.R.T.: 271 tonnes **Dimensions:** 29.14m x 9.98m x 4.41m **Machinery:** 2 Caterpillar diesels; 4,025 hp; 2 RR thrusters **Speed:** 13.1 knots **Complement:** 4 (Portsmouth); 5 (Clyde)

Notes: Azimuthing Tractor Drive (ATD) tugs. SD RELIABLE was built to a new design to provide assistance to warships and other vessels where exceptional manoeuvrability, precise control and adequate power are essential. Included in the design are a number of special features required specifically for use in the UK naval bases. Two double drum towing winches are fitted, along with extensive underwater fendering, fire fighting equipment and facilities for passenger and stores transportation. Construction of the hull and all major steel work for this vessel, and its three sisterships, was undertaken by a Damen subsidiary in Poland. SD BOUNTIFUL is based at Portsmouth. SD RESOURCE-FUL, SD RELIABLE and SD DEPENDABLE are based on the Clyde.

SD Faithful

TWIN UNIT TRACTOR TUGS

Ship	Completion Date	Builder
SD ADEPT	1980	Richard Dunston
SD CAREFUL	1982	Richard Dunston
SD FAITHFUL	1985	Richard Dunston
SD FORCEFUL	1985	Richard Dunston
SD POWERFUL	1985	Richard Dunston

G.R.T.: 384 tonnes **Dimensions:** 38.8m x 9.42m x 4m **Machinery:** 2 Ruston diesels; 2,575 hp; 2 Voith-Schneider propellers **Speed:** 12 knots **Complement:** 5

Notes: The principal harbour tugs in naval service. Some are to undergo a service life extension programme. All based at Devonport.

SD Hercules

STAN TUG 2608 CLASS

Ship	Completion Date	Builder
SD HERCULES	2009	Damen (Netherlands)
SD JUPITER	2009	Damen (Netherlands)
SD MARS	2009	Damen (Netherlands)

G.R.T.: 133.92 tonnes Dimensions: 26.61m x 8.44m x 4.05m Machinery: 2 Caterpillar 3508B TA diesels; 2,200 hp; 2 Van de Giessen Optima nozzles; 90kW HRP hydraulically powered bow thruster Speed: 12 knots Complement: 4 (6 max)

Notes: The Stan Tug has proved to be a popular and versatile conventional twin-screw tug for coastal and port operations. For naval service the tug has a comprehensive outfit of equipment to fit it for a wide variety of tasks in addition to towage operations in port and at sea. Two towing winches are fitted, a combined anchor windlass and single drum winch is located on the foredeck and a double drum towing winch on the after deck. These tugs have a particularly spacious after deck particularly suitable for handling submarine mounted towed sonar arrays. Bollard pull of 29.5 tonnes. SD HERCULES is based at Devonport and SD JUPITER on the Clyde. SD MARS now at Kyle of Lochalsh replaced SD MELTON where she also provides passenger capability but with added value as a towage asset.

• DEREK FOX

SD Suzanne

ASD 2009 CLASS

Ship	Completion Date	Builder
SD CHRISTINA	2010	Damen (Poland)
SD DEBORAH	2010	Damen (Poland)
SD EILEEN	2010	Damen (Poland)
SD SUZANNE	2010	Damen (Poland)

G.R.T.: 120.74 tonnes Dimensions: 21.2m x 9.4m x 3.9m Machinery: 2 Caterpillar 3508B TA/C diesels; 2,000 hp; 2 Rolls Royce US 155CP thrusters Speed: 11 knots Complement: 5

Notes: These Azimuth Stern Drive tugs are derived from the successful Damen ASD 2411 shiphandling tug. Winches fore and aft, together with a bow thruster, make these tugs suitable for handling smaller surface ships, barge work and assisting with submarine movements. SD DEBORAH and SD EILEEN are based at Devonport, SD CHRISTINA and SD SUZANNE at Portsmouth. Bollard pull 30 tonnes.

SD Helen

FELICITY CLASS

Ship	Completion Date	Builder
SD FLORENCE	1980	Richard Dunston
SD FRANCES	1980	Richard Dunstonn
SD GENEVIEVE	1980	Richard Dunston
SD HELEN	1974	Richard Dunston

G.R.T.: 88.96 tonnes **Dimensions:** 22.0m x 6.4m x 2.6m **Machinery:** 1 Mirrlees-Blackstone diesel; 615 hp; 1 Voith-Schneider CP propeller **Speed:** 10 knots **Complement:** 4 (Florence - 3)

Notes: The Felicity-class of water tractors (or tug boats) are used for the movement of small barges and equipment. SD FLORENCE is based at Devonport with SD GENEVIEVE and SD HELEN at Portsmouth. SD FRANCES is laid up at Devonport awaiting release from contract after which she will be put up for sale. Bollard pull 5.7 tonnes.

SD Catherine

PUSHY CAT 1204

Ship	Completion Date	Builder
SD CATHERINE	2008	Damen (Netherlands)
SD EMILY	2008	Damen (Netherlands)

G.R.T.: 29.4 tonnes **Dimensions:** 12.3m x 4.13m x 1.55m **Machinery:** 1 Caterpillar diesel; 165 hp; 1 shaft **Speed:** 8 knots **Complement:** 2

Notes: Powered by a single Caterpillar 3056 TA diesel driving a single screw. A propulsion nozzle is fitted and twin rudders to give a 2.1 tonnes bollard pull. They are used as general line runner and harbour workboat. SD CATHERINE is based at Portsmouth while SD EMILY is laid up at Devonport awaiting sale.

SD Tilly

STAN TUG 1405

Ship	Completion Date	Builder
SD TILLY	2009	Damen (Netherlands)

G.R.T.: 45 tonnes   **Dimensions:** 14.55m x 4.98m x 1.8m   **Machinery:** 2 Caterpillar diesels; 600 hp; 2 Van de Giessen nozzles   **Speed:** 9 knots   **Complement:** 3

Notes: A general purpose inshore and harbour tug based at Devonport. A twin screw version of the Pushy Cat 1204. Slightly larger with a bow thruster and also developing 8 tonnes bollard pull. Line handler, general workboat and ideal for moving small barges.

SD Victoria

WORLDWIDE SUPPORT VESSEL

Ship	Completion Date	Builder
SD VICTORIA	2010	Damen (Romania)

G.R.T.: 3,522 tonnes Dimensions: 83m x 16m x 4.5m Machinery: 2 Caterpillar diesels; 4,000 hp; 2 shafts; CP propellers; 1 bow thruster Speed: 14 knots Complement: 16 (accommodation for 72)

Notes: Built in Galatz (Romania) in 2010 the 83m training and support ship is the second largest vessel operated by Serco Marine Services in the UK and is based at Greenock's Great Harbour in Scotland. Powered by two Caterpillar 3516B diesels driving two shafts with controllable pitch propellers SD VICTORIA is designed to support training operations around the world. She is available for commercial charter and is primarily used to support military training and exercises as part of Serco's contract with the UK Ministry of Defence. She is equipped with classrooms, briefing rooms and operations rooms in addition to workshop facilities. There is provision to carry and operate RIBs and there is a helicopter winching deck.

SD Warden

TRIALS VESSEL

Ship	Completion Date	Builder
SD WARDEN	1989	Richards

Displacement: 626 tonnes **Dimensions:** 49m x 11m x 4m **Machinery:** 2 Ruston diesels; 4,000 hp; 2 shafts; CP propellers **Speed:** 15 knots **Complement:** 11

Notes: SD WARDEN was built in 1989 by Richards of Lowestoft as a Range Maintenance Vessel. She is based at Kyle of Lochalsh and functions as a Mooring and Weapons Recovery vessel owned and operated by Serco Marine and contracted to assist the Royal Navy. The harbour at Kyle of Lochalsh is a logistics base for vessels that support the work at the nearby British Underwater Test and Evaluation Centre (BUTEC) which is engaged in underwater weapons trials, sonar development and testing vessels noise signatures. She supports QinetiQ and the RN with experimental and trials work. She is the host vessel for Remotely Operated Vehicles (ROVs) and is also used to recover torpedoes. SD WARDEN is to remain in service until 2022.

SD Kyle of Lochalsh

TRIALS VESSEL

Ship	Completion Date	Builder
SD KYLE OF LOCHALSH	1997	Abels Boatbuilders

Displacement: 120 tonnes   **Dimensions:** 24.35m x 9m x 3.45m   **Machinery:** 2 Caterpillar diesels; 2,992 hp; 2 shafts   **Speed:** 10.5 knots   **Complement:** 4

Notes: The former twin-screw tug boat MCS LENIE was built in 1997 by Abels Boatbuilders in Bristol. She had been under contract to the MOD in Scotland for some time before she was purchased from Maritime Craft Services (Clyde) Ltd by Serco Marine Services and renamed SD KYLE OF LOCHALSH in 2008. She is used to support trials and operations at Kyle of Lochalsh. Bollard pull 26 tonnes.

SD Bovisand

TENDERS
STORM CLASS

Ship	Completion Date	Builder
SD BOVISAND	1997	FBM (Cowes)
SD CAWSAND	1997	FBM (Cowes)

G.R.T.: 225 tonnes **Dimensions:** 23m x 11m x 2m **Machinery:** 2 Caterpillar diesels; 1,224 hp; 2 shafts **Speed:** 15 knots **Complement:** 5

Notes: These craft are used in support of Flag Officer Sea Training (FOST) at Plymouth to transfer staff quickly and comfortably to and from Warships and Auxiliaries within and beyond the Plymouth breakwater in open sea conditions. These were the first vessels of a small waterplane area twin hull (SWATH) design ordered by the Ministry of Defence and cost £6.5 million each. Speed restrictions were implemented due to wash problems generated by these vessels. They are to remain in service until 2022.

RAYMOND WERGAN

SD Newhaven

NEWHAVEN CLASS

Ship	Completion Date	Builder
SD NEWHAVEN	2000	Aluminium SB
SD NUTBOURNE	2000	Aluminium SB
SD NETLEY	2001	Aluminium SB

Displacement: 77 tonnes (45 grt) Dimensions: 18.3m x 6.8m x 1.88m Machinery: 2 Cummins diesels; 710 hp; 2 shafts Speed: 10 knots Complement: 2/3 Crew (60 passengers)

Notes: These MCA Class IV Passenger Vessels were acquired as replacements for Fleet tenders. Employed on general passenger duties within the port area. SD NETLEY and SD NUTBOURNE are based at Portsmouth, SD NEWHAVEN is based at Devonport and operates in support of Flag Officer Sea Training (FOST). She has undergone modifications to strengthen her forward bollard and add transfer wings to enable underway personnel transfers with some classes of vessel undertaking sea training. They are all to remain in service until 2022.

SD Padstow

PADSTOW CLASS

Ship	Completion Date	Builder
SD PADSTOW	2000	Aluminium SB

Displacement: 77 tonnes (45 grt) **Dimensions:** 18.3m x 6.8m x 1.88m **Machinery:** 2 Cummins diesels; 710 hp; 2 shafts **Speed:** 10 knots **Complement:** 2/3 Crew (60 passengers)

Notes: SD PADSTOW was constructed by Aluminium Shipbuilders in Hampshire. The MCA Class IV, VI and VIA Passenger Vessel is based at Devonport. Used on liberty runs in Plymouth Sound and the Harbour as well as occasionally supporting FOST. Has undergone similar modifications as SD NEWHAVEN (previous page) in order to conduct underway personnel transfers. She is to remain in service until 2022.

SD Oban

OBAN CLASS

Ship	Completion Date	Builder
SD OBAN	2000	McTay Marine
SD ORONSAY	2000	McTay Marine
SD OMAGH	2000	McTay Marine

G.R.T.: 199 tonnes **Dimensions:** 27.7m x 7.30m x 3.75m **Machinery:** 2 Cummins diesels; 1,050 hp; 2 Kort-nozzles **Speed:** 10 knots **Complement:** 4 Crew (60 passengers)

Notes: The three Oban-class tenders (MCA Class IIA Passenger Vessels) replaced the Fleet tenders in 2001. The lead ship of the class, SD-OBAN, was originally based on the Clyde but was transferred to Devonport in 2003 and is now primarily used to support FOST staff. The other two, SD ORONSAY and SD OMAGH are employed on general passenger duties on the Clyde and are additionally classified as Cargo Ship VIII(A). All three are to remain in service until 2022.

SD Norton

PERSONNEL FERRY

Ship	Completion Date	Builder
SD NORTON	1989	FBM Marine

G.R.T.: 21 tonnes **Dimensions:** 15.8m x 5.5m x 1.5m **Machinery:** 2 Mermaid Turbo diesels; 280 hp; 2 shafts **Speed:** 13 knots **Complement:** 2

Notes: SD Norton is a single FBM catamaran, 8837, operating at Portsmouth. She can carry 30 passengers or 2 tonnes of stores. She was designed as a prototype personnel launch catamaran designed to replace older Harbour Launches but no more were ordered.

● JOHN CRAE

SD Eva

PERSONNEL FERRY

Ship	Completion Date	Builder
SD EVA	2009	Damen (Netherlands)

G.R.T.: 168 tonnes **Dimensions:** 33.5m x 7.36m x 3.3m **Machinery:** 2 Caterpillar diesels; 2,800 hp; 2 shafts **Speed:** 30 knots **Complement:** 4-6 (plus 34 passengers)

Notes: SD EVA operates on the Clyde as a Fast Crew Transport to transfer crew to and from military vessels. The Axe Bow design allows the vessel to effectively cut through waves with minimal movement of the vessel. The vessel is the first of its type in the UK to be operated under the International Code of Safety for High Speed Craft (HSC Code). She is no longer on contract having been released in 2016. Although still owned by Serco she remains laid up in Greenock awaiting sale.

SD Melton

FLEET TENDERS

Ship	Completion Date	Builder
SD MELTON	1981	Richard Dunston
SD MENAI	1981	Richard Dunston
SD MEON	1982	Richard Dunston

G.R.T.: 117.3 tonnes **Dimensions:** 24m x 6.7m x 3.05m **Machinery:** 1 Lister Blackstone diesel; 320 hp; 1 shaft **Speed:** 10.5 knots **Complement:** 4 (12 passengers)

Notes: The last three survivors of a once numerous class of vessels used as Training Tenders, Passenger Ferries or Cargo Vessels. MENAI and MEON are still operated at Falmouth. A vessel replacement programme now seems unlikely and this elderly pair are expected to remain in service until 2022. MELTON was released from contract and put up for sale. Her role has been taken over by MARS. She was acquired by Edinburgh-based medical-oriented charity Vine Trust which intends to operate her as a medical vessel complete with consultation rooms, a dental clinic, an operating room, a laboratory and a pharmacy. Over the next 12 to 18 months she is set to undergo conversion work prior to being deployed on medical missions overseas.

COASTAL OILER

Ship	Completion Date	Builder
SD TEESDALE	1976	Yorkshire Drydock Co.

G.R.T.: 499 tonnes **Dimensions:** 43.86m x 9.5m x 3.92m **Speed:** 8 knots **Complement:** 5

Notes: Formerly the oil products tanker TEESDALE H operated by John H Whitaker. Operates as a parcel tanker delivering diesel and aviation fuel and also delivering/receiving compensating water. She is self-propelled by two Aquamaster thrusters. A Diesel Lighter Barge, SD OILMAN, and a Water Lighter Barge, SD WATER-PRESS, are operated on the Clyde. A further barge, a Liquid Mixed Lighter Barge, SD OCEANSPRAY, is based at Portsmouth.

SD Northern River

MULTI-PURPOSE VESSEL

Ship	Completion Date	Builder
SD NORTHERN RIVER	1998	Myklebust (Norway)

G.R.T.: 3,605 tonnes Dimensions: 92.8m x 18.8m x 4.9m Machinery: 2 Bergen diesels; 9,598 hp; 2 shafts; CP propellers; 2 bow thrusters Speed: 14 knots Complement: 14

Notes: SD NORTHERN RIVER is currently the largest multi-purpose auxiliary ship operated by Serco Marine Services, both in terms of dimensions and gross tonnage. She was bought from Deep Ocean AS (a subsidiary of Trico Marine). The Ulstein UT-745L designed Support Vessel entered service with Serco in March 2012. She can be employed on a variety of tasking from target towing, through noise ranging to data gathering; boarding training to submarine escort. Her extensive flat work deck allows her to embark containers for passive sonar training. She can also provide nuclear emergency support as well as support to submarine emergencies. She can provide mother ship training facilities for the NATO Submarine Rescue System (NSRS), which involves the embarkation, fitting and operation of specialist ROV's, escape vessels and Transfer Under Pressure (TUP) facilities on the after deck, together with the embarkation of up to 40 additional personnel. She can also support the Submarine Parachute Assistance Group.

MICHAEL LENNON

DIVING SUPPORT VESSELS
MOOR CLASS

Ship	Completion Date	Builder
SD MOORFOWL	1989	McTay Marine
SD MOORHEN	1989	McTay Marine

Displacement: 518 tonnes **Dimensions:** 36m x 12m x 2m **Machinery:** 2 Cummins diesels; 796 hp; 2 Aquamasters; 1 bow thruster **Speed:** 8 knots **Complement:** 10

Notes: Designed as a powered mooring lighter for use within sheltered coastal waters the lifting horns have been removed from the bows of both vessels when they were converted to Diving Support Vessels. They are used by the Defence Diving School for diving training in the Kyle of Lochalsh. In January 2016 SD MOORHEN had a main engine and generator overhaul. During this time, the Aquamaster propulsion unit was also overhauled, which involved removing the port unit for work at Rolls Royce. She also had a hull UT survey, steelwork repairs, HP wash and paint were carried out and its tank was cleaned, coated and certified to finish. Both vessels are to remain in service until 2022.

RAYMOND WERGAN

SD Navigator

MULTICAT 2510 CLASS

Ship	Completion Date	Builder
SD NAVIGATOR	2009	Damen (Netherlands)
SD RAASAY	2010	Damen (Netherlands)

Displacement: 362 tonnes   Dimensions: 25.54m x 10.64m x 2.34m   Machinery: 2 Caterpillar diesels; 957 hp; 2 shafts Speed: 8.4 knots Complement: 3 (plus up to 12 additional personnel)

Notes: SD NAVIGATOR is equipped for buoy handling with a single 9 tonnes capacity crane. She is capable of supporting diving operations. SD RAASAY is based at the Kyle of Lochalsh and is fitted with two cranes for torpedo recovery and support diving training. SD NAVIGATOR is managed from Devonport but operates between Devonport and Portsmouth. Two similar vessels, SD INSPECTOR (ex-DMS EAGLE) and SD ENGINEER, operate from Portsmouth and Devonport respectively.

SD Angeline

MULTICAT 2613 CLASS

Ship	Completion Date	Builder
SD ANGELINE	2015	Damen (Netherlands)

Displacement: 657 tonnes **Dimensions:** 25.5m x 13.6m x 4m **Machinery:** 2 Caterpillar C32 TTA diesels; 2 Promarin fixed pitch propellers; bow thruster **Speed:** 10.1 knots **Complement:** Accommodation for 8 persons, consisting of four double crew cabins

Notes: Her total power output is 2,850 kW with a bollard pull of 30.8 tonnes. The crane has a capacity of 15 tonnes. Ordered in April 2014 she was accepted by the MoD in April 2015. Built at the request of the MoD to provide support in Faslane Naval Base primarily to submarines, but can undertake other naval base work.

SD Solent Racer

STAN TENDER 1505 CLASS

Ship	Completion Date	Builder
SD CLYDE RACER	2008	Damen (Netherlands)
SD SOLENT RACER	2008	Damen (Netherlands)
SD TAMAR RACER	2008	Damen (Netherlands)

G.R.T.: 25.19 tonnes **Dimensions:** 15.2m x 4.8m x 1.3m **Machinery:** 2 Caterpillar diesels; 1,100 hp; 2 shafts **Speed:** 26 knots **Complement:** 2 (+ 8 Passengers)

Notes: Of aluminium construction these boats are employed on transfer of pilots, port security operations and VIP and passenger transportation.

● DEREK FOX

SD Solent Spirit

STAN TENDER 1905 CLASS

Ship	Completion Date	Builder
SD CLYDE SPIRIT	2008	Damen (Netherlands)
SD SOLENT SPIRIT	2008	Damen (Netherlands)
SD TAMAR SPIRIT	2008	Damen (Netherlands)

G.R.T.: 43.3 tonnes Dimensions: 19.2m x 5.3m x 1.8m Machinery: 2 Caterpillar diesels; 2,200 hp; 2 shafts Speed: 25 knots Complement: 2 (+ 10 passengers)

Notes: Steel hull with aluminium superstructure. Special propeller tunnels are fitted to increase propulsion efficiency and to reduce vibration and noise levels. These vessels are able to operate safely and keep good performance in wind speeds up to Force 6 and wave heights of 2 metres. Employed on transfer of pilots, VIPs and personnel.

SD Kingdom of Fife

ANCHOR HANDLING TUG

Ship	Completion Date	Builder
KINGDOM OF FIFE	2008	Damen (Romania)

Displacement: 1,459 tonnes **Dimensions:** 61.2m x 13.5m x 4.75m **Machinery:** 2 Caterpillar diesels, 2,720 hp each; 1 shaft; bow thruster **Speed:** 13.7 knots **Complement:** 18

Notes: Briggs Marine won a £100m contract from Serco to support navigation buoy maintenance and mooring support for the Royal Navy for 15 years. During the contract period, Briggs Marine provide support for over 350 moorings, navigation buoys and targets for the RN all around the UK coast, as well as Cyprus, Gibraltar and the Falkland Islands. KINGDOM OF FIFE was delivered in May 2008 and supports the existing Briggs Marine shallow draught and heavy lift craft CAMERON in servicing the contract and can be equipped with a decompression chamber with support from the Serco dive team.

● LEE HARRISON   **SD Cameron**

● LEE HARRISON

Smit Dee

AIRCREW TRAINING VESSELS

Ship	Comp Date	Builder	Base Port
SMIT DEE	2003	BES Rosyth	Buckie
SMIT DART	2003	BES Rosyth	Plymouth
SMIT DON	2003	BES Rosyth	Blyth
SMIT YARE	2003	FBMA Cebu	Great Yarmouth
SMIT SPEY	2003	FBMA Cebu	Plymouth

G.R.T.: 95.86 GRT **Dimensions:** 27.6m x 6.6m x 1.5m **Machinery:** 2 Cummins diesels; 1,400 hp; 2 shafts; 1 centreline waterjet; 305hp **Speed:** 20 knots **Complement:** 6

Notes: The service for Marine Support to Range Safety and Aircrew Training is provided by SMIT International (Scotland) Ltd. A new seven year contract for £39M started in April 2018 and will run for five years until March 2023, with an option to extend for a further two years. These vessels provide support to aircrew training such as sea survival drills, various helicopter exercises, target towing and other general marine support tasks. They also participate in Navy Command sea training serials, particularly boarding exercises and force protection exercises involving fast attack craft scenarios. SMIT DART completed as a passenger vessel with a larger superstructure.

● LEE HARRISON

Smit Stour

RANGE SAFETY VESSELS

Ship	Comp Date	Builder
SMIT STOUR	2003	Maritime Partners Norway
SMIT ROTHER	2003	Maritime Partners Norway
SMIT ROMNEY	2003	Maritime Partners Norway
SMIT CERNE	2003	Maritime Partners Norway
SMIT FROME	2003	Maritime Partners Norway
SMIT MERRION	2003	Maritime Partners Norway
SMIT PENALLY	2003	Maritime Partners Norway
SMIT WEY	2003	Maritime Partners Norway
SMIT NEYLAND	2003	Maritime Partners Norway

G.R.T.: 7.0 GRT **Dimensions:** 12.3m x 2.83m x 0.89m **Machinery:** 2 Volvo Penta diesels; 680 hp; 2 Hamilton waterjets **Speed:** 28 knots **Complement:** 2

Notes: A class of 12m Fast Patrol Craft which provide a range safety service to 7 land based ranges across the UK. They also participate in Navy Command Sea Training serials including participation in Fast Attack Craft scenarios. Part of £39 million contract the MoD awarded to SMIT International (Scotland) Ltd in April 2018.

AWB Mistral

ARMY VESSELS
WORK BOATS

Vessel	Pennant Number	Completion Date	Builder
STORM	WB41	2008	Warbreck Eng.
DIABLO	WB42	2008	Warbreck Eng.
MISTRAL	WB43	2008	Warbreck Eng.
SIROCCO	WB44	2008	Warbreck Eng.

Displacement: 48 tonnes **Dimensions:** 14.75m x 4.30m **Machinery:** 2 John Deere Diesels; 402 hp; 2 shafts **Speed:** 10 knots **Complement:** 4

Notes: Part of the Army's strategic port operations in Southampton, but can be transported by a 'mother ship' to other ports and places like Iraq. Are often used as tugs for mexeflotes, positioning other pontoon equipment and for handling flexible pipelines. They have a firefighting capability. The Army also operate a number of smaller Combat Support Boats. Built by RTK Marine/VT Halmatic (now BAE) these are fast and rugged small craft, 8.8m long with a twin Hamilton waterjet propulsion system powered by twin 210hp diesel engines.

HMC Vigilant

BORDER FORCE
STAN PATROL 4207 CLASS

Vessel	Callsign	Completion Date	Builder
SEARCHER	ZQNK9	2002	Damen
SEEKER	ZQNL2	2001	Damen
VALIANT	MBLL8	2004	Damen
VIGILANT	ZITI4	2003	Damen

G.R.T.: 238 tonnes **Dimensions:** 42.8m x 7.11m x 2.52m **Machinery:** 2 Caterpillar 3516B diesels, 2 shafts; 2 4-blade controllable pitch propellers; 1 Promac bow thruster **Speed:** 26+ knots **Complement:** 12

Notes: These vessels are able to remain at sea for extended periods and in heavy weather conditions. They operate 24 hours a day, 365 days per year, through the employment of dual crews. There are ten crews for the five Border Force cutters comprising 120 seago-ing staff, working two weeks on and two weeks off. Cutters are mostly deployed on a risk-led or intelligence-led basis detecting prohibited and restricted goods, boarding and searching ships and providing a law enforcement presence in remote and inaccessible areas. Vessels are prefixed HMC for Her Majesty's Cutter. They were built at the Damen Shipyard in the Netherlands and all have a steel hull with an aluminium superstructure. All are based at Portsmouth.

MICHEL FLOCH

HMC Protector

TELKKÄ CLASS

Vessel	Callsign	Completion Date	Builder
PROTECTOR	2GWY9	2002	UKI Workboat

Displacement: 434 tonnes Dimensions: 49.7m x 7.3m x 3.65m Machinery: 2 Wärtsilä 12V200 diesels, 7,240 hp; 2 shafts; CP propeller; bow and stern thrusters Speed: 22 knots Complement: 12

Notes: Acquired in August 2013 (and commissioned in March 2014) she is the former Finnish Border Agency vessel TAVI. Twice deployed to the Mediterranean (alongside HMC SEEKER) as part of Operation Triton, led by Frontex, the EU's external border control agency. There she conducted search and rescue operations and helped in tackling the criminal gangs that are responsible for illegal attempts to move large numbers of migrants across the Mediterranean. Both vessels worked together with the Italian Armed Forces and PROTECTOR had a small contingent of Royal Marines aboard.

● DEREK FOX

Alert

DELTA ARRC 190 CLASS

Vessel	Callsign	Completion Date	Builder
EAGLE	ZCPH5	2006	Holyhead Marine/Delta ARCC
NIMROD	2JQP9	2006	Holyhead Marine/Delta ARCC
ALERT	2JQQ2	2006	Holyhead Marine/Delta ARCC
ACTIVE	2JQQ3	2006	Holyhead Marine/Delta ARCC
HUNTER	ZCOO3	2006	Holyhead Marine/Delta ARCC
SPEEDWELL		2006	Holyhead Marine/Delta ARCC
ASTUTE		2006	Holyhead Marine/Delta ARCC
ARDENT		2006	Holyhead Marine/Delta ARCC

Displacement: 29 GRT Dimensions: 17.75m x 5.63m x 0.9m Machinery: 2 Caterpillar C18 diesels, 1,000 hp; 2 Hamilton waterjets Speed: 34 knots Complement: 6

Notes: Starting in 2016, to boost the number of vessels patrolling the UK coastline, eight ex-BP Project Jigsaw rescue craft, built by Holyhead Marine (Holyhead) and Delta ARCC (Stockport), were acquired by Border Force. They are termed Coastal Patrol Vessels within Border Force. As well as carrying out regular patrols of UK waters, CPVs will act on intelligence provided by law enforcement and international partners. Callsigns are displayed on superstructure roof forward of the bridge. The design includes a deep-vee fibre-reinforced plastic hull design and can return to the upright position if capsized.

AIRCRAFT & UNITS

NAVY COMMAND SQUADRONS

814 NAS*	Merlin HM2	TAG/RNAS Culdrose
815 NAS	Wildcat HMA2	Flights/RNAS Yeovilton
820 NAS	Merlin HM2	TAG/RNAS Culdrose
824 NAS	Merlin HM2	Training/RNAS Culdrose
825 NAS	Wildcat HMA2	Training/RNAS Yeovilton
849 NAS	Sea King ASaC7	TAG/RNAS Culdrose
	Merlin HM2 'Crowsnest'	Forming
727 NAS	Tutor T1	Grading/RNAS Yeovilton
736 NAS	Hawk T1	FOST/RNAS Culdrose
FOST Flight	Dauphin 2	HMNB Devonport

JOINT FORCE LIGHTNING

17 Sqn	F-35B Lightning II	Edwards AFB - USA
617 Sqn	F-35B Lightning II	TAG/RAF Marham
207 Sqn	F-35B Lightning II (projected)	Training/RAF Marham

JOINT HELICOPTER COMMAND

845 NAS	Merlin HC4/3i	TAG/RNAS Yeovilton
846 NAS	Merlin HC4/3i	TAG/RNAS Yeovilton
847 NAS	Wildcat AH1	TAG/RNAS Yeovilton
7 Sqn	Chinook HC4/4A/5	TAG/RAF Odiham
18 Sqn	Chinook HC4/4A/5	TAG/RAF Odiham
27 Sqn	Chinook HC4/4A/5	TAG/RAF Odiham
28(AC) Sqn	Chinook HC4/4A/5	Training/RAF Odiham
1 Regt.	Wildcat AH1	TAG/RNAS Yeovilton
3 Regt.	Apache AH1	TAG/AAC Wattisham
4 Regt.	Apache AH1	TAG/AAC Wattisham

MILITARY FLYING TRAINING SYSTEM

4(R) Sqn	Hawk T2	4 FTS/RAF Valley
72(R) Sqn	Tucano T1	1 FTS/RAF Linton-on-Ouse
703 Sqn	Tutor T1	3 FTS/RAF Barkston Heath
750 NAS	Avenger T1	RNAS Culdrose
705 Sqn	Juno HT1	DHFS/RAF Shawbury

*At the end of March 2018 829 Naval Air Squadron decommissioned and merged with 814 NAS.

● CROWN COPYRIGHT/MOD

Leonardo Helicopters MERLIN HM2

Role: Anti-submarine search and strike; maritime surveillance
Engines: 3 x Rolls Royce/Turbomeca RTM 322 each developing 2,100 shp
Length: 74' 10" **Rotor:** diameter 61' **Height:** 21' 10"
Max. Weight: 32,120lb **Max. Speed:** 167 knots **Crew:** 1/2 pilots, 1 observer, 1 aircrewman
Avionics: Blue Kestrel radar; Orange Reaper ESM; Folding Light Acoustic System for helicopters (FLASH); AQS-903 acoustic processor; Wescam MX-15 electro-optical/IR camera; defensive aids including Directional Infrared Countermeasures (DIRCM), AN/AAR-57 radar warning system, chaff and flare dispensers;
Armament: Up to 4 Stingray torpedoes or Mark 11 depth charges; 1 x M3M 0.5" machine-gun in cabin door and 1 x 7.62mm machine-gun in cabin window

Squadron Service: 814, 820, 824, 849 Naval Air Squadrons

Notes: At the end of March 2018 829 Naval Air Squadron decommissioned and merged with 814 NAS to create the biggest Merlin Mk2 helicopter Squadron that the Royal Navy has ever had. This might signal the start of the execution of the MoD forward plan which showed 820 NAS allocated for carrier embarkation between 2018 - 2026 and 814 (and now 829) NAS specialising in providing aircraft for RFAs and frigates. There is still the chance that the merged 814 NAS might be absorbed into 820 NAS in due course.824 NAS is the training unit for all anti-submarine aircrew, ASaC 'Crowsnest' and commando Merlin pilots. 'Crowsnest' fitted Merlins in which anti-submarine role equipment can be replaced by ASaC sensors and consoles are being delivered by Leonardo helicopters and sufficient should have been received for IOC to be achieved in 2020. ASaC observer training will be carried out by the HQ Flight of 849 NAS and operational aircraft will be allocated to TAGs from 2021. In the future the Merlin Mk2, as part of the the Crowsnest programme, will also be the replacement aircraft for the Navy's Sea King Mk7 Airborne Surveillance and Control.

Leonardo Helicopters WILDCAT HMA2

Roles: Surface search and strike; anti-submarine strike; boarding party support
Engines: 2 x LHTEC CTS 800 each developing 1,362 shp
Length: 50' **Rotor diameter:** 42' **Height:** 12'
Max. Weight: 13,200lb **Max. Speed:** 157 knots **Crew:** 1 pilot & 1 observer
Avionics: Selex-Galileo Sea Spray 7400E multi-mode AESA radar; Wescam MX-15 electro-optical/IR camera; Electronic warfare system and defensive aids suite. Bowman communications system
Armament: 2 x Stingray torpedoes or Mark 11 depth charges; 1 x M3M 0.5" machine-gun in cabin door. From 2020 to carry Martlet (light) and Sea Venom (heavy) air-to-surface guided weapons.

Squadron Service: 815, 825 Naval Air Squadrons

Notes: 825 NAS is the training and tactical development unit and 815 NAS deploys flights of 1 or 2 aircraft to destroyers, frigates that do not embark Merlins and some RFAs. Wildcat is designed around a digital avionics management system that enhances mission effectiveness and reduces aircrew workload. Its 'paperless' maintenance system is shared with the Wildcat AH 1 operated by the Joint Helicopter Command. With the Lynx HMA 8 withdrawn from service in 2017, Wildcats now fully equip these two naval air squadrons which are both shore-based at RNAS Yeovilton. The HMA 2 is to have a significant strike capability when the Martlet and Sea Venom air-to-surface guided weapons achieve initial operational capability after 2020. With the withdrawal from service of 700X NAS ScanEagle detachments in 2017, Wildcats and Merlins are the only air assets capable of deployment in destroyers, frigates and RFAs.

● DANIEL FERRO

BAE Systems HAWK T1

Role: Threat simulation aircraft
Engine: 1 x Rolls Royce Adour 151 delivering 5,200lb of thrust.
Length: 40' 9" **Wingspan:** 32' 7" **Height:** 13' 1"
Max. Weight: 20,000lb **Max. Speed:** Mach 0.88 (Mach 1.2 in a dive) **Crew:** 1 or 2 pilots
Avionics: standard communications fit
Armament: Can be fitted with a 30mm gun pod on a centreline pylon and one pylon under each wing capable of taking AIM-9 Sidewinder or up to 1,500lb of practice weapons

Squadron Service: 736 Naval Air Squadron

Notes: 736 NAS is the focal point for fixed-wing flying standards and practices within the Navy Command structure and provides continuity flying for pilots destined to be fed into the F-35B Lightning II training programme. It also provides aircraft for fighter controller and ASaC observer training plus attack simulations for FOST activities and 'Joint Warrior' exercises, effectively acting as an RN 'aggressor unit'. 'The aircraft are maintained by Babcock, regularly operated from both RN Air Stations Culdrose and Yeovilton and frequently deploy in support of exercises and fleet deployments. Under current plans 736 NAS' Hawk T1s are due to be withdrawn from service in 2020 although T1s operated by Air Command, including those flown by the Red Arrows display team, are expected to run on for longer. The MoD has made no statement about replacement options.

Grob TUTOR T1

Role: Elementary training
Engine: 1 x Textron Lycoming AE10-360-B1F developing 180 shp
Length: 24' 9" **Wingspa:n** 32' 9" **Height:** 7'
Max. Weight: 2,178lb **Max. Speed:** 185 knots **Crew:** 2 pilots
Avionics: None
Armament: None

Squadron Service: 727 Naval Air Squadron, 703 Squadron MFTS

Notes: Tutors are used within Navy Command for the grading of potential aircrew and, in the short term to clear a backlog in the MFTS, it provides elementary flying training for up to 12 student pilots per year. 703 Squadron is not a naval air squadron although it is numbered in what was until recently an exclusively naval sequence. It is part of the MFTS, providing elementary pilot training at RAF Barkston Heath for RN and RM pilots and Phase 1 and 2 training for RN observers.

F-35B on HMS Queen Elizabeth

Lockheed Martin F-35B LIGHTNING II

Role: Strike, fighter and reconnaissance aircraft

Engine: 1 X Pratt & Whitney F135-PW-600 delivering 41,000lb thrust with reheat in conventional flight; 40,650lb hover thrust with Rolls-Royce lift fan engaged and tail nozzle rotated.

Length: 51' 4"   **Wingspan:** 35'   **Height:** 15'

Max. Weight: 60,000lb **Max. Speed:** Mach 1.6 **Crew:** 1 pilot

Avionics: AN/APG-81 AESA radar; AN/AAQ-40 electro-optical targeting system; AN/AAQ-37 distributed aperture system; AN/ASQ-239 'Barracuda' electronic warfare system; pilot's helmet-mounted display system; multi-function advanced data link.

Armament: Current Block 2B software allows the stealthy carriage of weapons in 2 internal bays with a single ASRAAM or AMRAAM air-to-air missile plus a single 1,000lb bomb equivalent such as Paveway IV LGB in each. Block 3F software in operational aircraft delivered from 2017 will enable the additional use of 7 non-stealthy external pylons, 3 under each wing and 1 under the centreline. A total of 12,000lb of weapons or fuel tanks to be carried; inner wing pylons have 'plumbing' for 426 US gallon drop tanks.

Squadron Service 17, 207, 617 Squadrons.

Notes: By January 2018 the UK had taken delivery of 16 Lightnings II out of the 138 to be ordered and delivered in annual batches. In November 2018 the MoD announced that it had ordered another 17 new F-35Bs with delivery between 2020 and 2022. These new F-35Bs would complement the 16 aircraft currently based at RAF Marham (14) and in the US (2), as well as two additional aircraft which are already on order. The UK has committed to purchase a total of 138 aircraft from Lockheed Martin over the life of the programme. The F-35B is jointly operated by pilots from the Fleet Air Arm and the Royal Air Force. RN and RAF personnel of 617 Squadron trained with the US Marine Corps' VMFAT-501 Squadron at MCAS Beaufort and moved to RAF Marham where it formed officially in 2018. 809 Naval Air Squadron (NAS) has been resurrected as the first RN formation to operate the fifth generation stealth aircraft that will fly off the Royal Navy's Queen Elizabeth Class carriers. The F-35 is an Anglo-American joint effort and numerous British companies are part of the construction process. Around 25,000 British jobs are involved in the project and it is estimated that around £35 billion will be contributed to the UK economy. According to the RN 809 Naval Air Squadron was selected because of its history of striking at the enemy in operations across the globe. In previous incarnations, aircraft from 809 supported an attack on Hitler's flagship, supported the invasions of North Africa, Italy and southern France during World War 2 and saw action in the Suez in 1956. It was last re-formed to support operations in the Falklands, flying off the decks of HMS HERMES and HMS INVINCIBLE. 809 also flew the Navy's last Buccaneer, a low level strike bomber flown in the 1960s and 1970s. The joint nature of the Squadrons means Naval personnel will serve with The Dambusters and their Air Force counterparts will do likewise on 809 NAS.

● STEVE WRIGHT

Leonardo Helicopters MERLIN HC3, HC3i, HC4

Role: Commando assault, load-lifting, troop movement
Engines: 3 x Rolls Royce/Turbomeca RTM 322 each developing 2,100 shp
Length: 74' 10" **Rotor diameter:** 61' **Height:** 21' 10"
Max. Weight: 32,120lb **Max. Speed:** 167 knots **Crew:** 1 or 2 pilots, 1 aircrewman
Avionics: Wescam MX-15 electro-optical/IR camera; defensive aids suite including directional IR countermeasures, AN/AAR-57 missile approach warning system, automatic chaff and flare dispensers
Armament: 1 x M3M 0.5" machine-gun in cabin door; 1 x 7.62mm machine-gun in cabin window

Squadron Service: 845, 846 Naval Air squadrons.

Notes: The first of 25 Merlin HC3s to be modified to HC4 standard was delivered by Leonardo Helicopters in 2017 and the last is due to be delivered in 2020, restoring an embarked capability to the Commando Helicopter Force, CHF. 7 aircraft have been modified to an interim HC3i standard to give some TAG capability until sufficient HC4s are available. The HC4 has a 'glass cockpit' similar to that of the HM2, power-folding main rotor head and tail pylon together with improved communications and defensive aids. Unlike the green HC3s, Merlin HC4s are painted grey. 845 NAS is eventually to have 10 aircraft deployable in up to 3 TAGs and 846 NAS is also to have 10 with an operational conversion/training flight, a maritime counter-terrorism flight and, after 2020, a TAG flight to back up 845. The remaining 5 airframes give deep maintenance flexibility and will act as attrition reserves.

Leonardo Helicopters WILDCAT AH1

Role: Battlefield reconnaissance; airborne command and control, force protection and troop transport.
Engines: 2 x LHTEC CTS 800-4N turboshafts each developing 1,362 shp
Length: 50' **Rotor diameter:** 42' **Height:** 12'
Max. Weight: 13,200lb **Max. Speed:** 157 knots **Crew:** 2 pilots & 1 gunner
Avionics: L-3 Wescam MX-15Di electro-optical/laser designator turret; digital mission planning system; Selex HIDAS 15 electronic warfare system
Armament: Door-mounted 0.5 inch M3M machine gun.

Squadron Service: 847 Naval Air Squadron, 1 Regiment Army Air Corps

Notes: 847 NAS is shore-based at RNAS Yeovilton and operates the Wildcat AH 1 as part of the Commando Helicopter Force, within the Joint Helicopter Command, to support 3 Commando Brigade with battlefield reconnaissance and airborne command and control of forces on the ground. 1 Regiment is also based at RNAS Yeovilton and operates, effectively, as a joint force with the RN Wildcat squadrons. It comprises a headquarters squadron plus 652, 659 and 661 Squadrons which operate their Wildcats as a specialised intelligence, surveillance and reconnaissance aircraft in support of troops on the ground. In the troop-lift role, Army Wildcats can lift up to 5 fully-equipped troops over short distances. Like 847 NAS they can be embarked to form part of a TAG when required and AAC pilots are trained to operate from the sea.

Leonardo Helicopters APACHE AH1

Role: Attack and armed reconnaissance helicopter
Engines: 2 x Rolls Royce/Turbomeca RTM 322 turboshafts each developing 2,100 shp
Length: 58' 3" **Rotor diameter:** 17' 2" **Height:** 15' 3"
Max. Weight: 15,075lb **Max. Speed:** 150 knots **Crew:** 2 pilots
Avionics: Selex HIDAS defensive aids suite; Longbow radar; optical and infrared target indication sensors.
Armament: Up to 16 AGM-114 Hellfire air-to-surface guided weapons; up to 4 Sidewinder air-to-air missiles; M230 30mm cannon with 1,160 rounds; up to 76 CRV-7 unguided air-to-surface missiles.

Squadron Service: 3 and 4 Regiments Army Air Corps

Notes: 3 Regiment AAC comprises 653, 662 and 663 Squadrons. 4 Regiment comprises 656 and 664 Squadrons and both formations are based at the AAC base at Wattisham and form part of the Joint Helicopter Command. Apaches of 656 Squadron flew successfully on operations over Libya with a TAG embarked in OCEAN during 2011 and at least one unit is maintained at high readiness for embarked operations as part of a TAG but in an emergency a larger number of Apaches could be embarked if required.

Boeing CHINOOK HC4, HC4A and HC5

Role: Battlefield transport helicopter
Engines: 2 x Avco Lycoming T55-L-712 turboshafts each developing 3,750 shp
Length: 98' 9" **Rotor diameter:** 60' **Height:** 18' 8"
Max. weight: 50,000lb **Max. speed:** 160 knots **Crew:** 2 pilots & 2 aircrewmen/gunners
Avionics: Infrared jammer; missile warning system; integrated digital 'glass cock-pit'; moving map tablet and improved crewman's work station.
Armament: up to 2 M 134 mini guns mounted in doorways; one M 60 machine gun on rear loading ramp.

Squadron Service: 7, 18, 27, 28(AC) Squadrons Royal Air Force

Notes: All 4 squadrons are based at RAF Odiham from where the 3 operational units can provide TAG detachments when required. The Chinook's rotor blades cannot fold but QUEEN ELIZABETH's side lifts are large enough to strike down the aircraft, fully spread, into the hangar and they can be embarked in significant numbers to support both amphibious military and humanitarian operations. Chinooks can carry 54 fully-equipped troops, 24 stretcher cases or loads up to 44,000lb carried both internally and externally over short distances. With extra fuel tanks they have a range of 1,000nm with a light load. Originally designed for the US Army, Chinooks are in wide-spread service throughout the world. The first model flew in 1961.

MILITARY FLYING TRAINING SYSTEM
The aircraft used to train RN & RM pilots and observers

● STEVE WRIGHT

BAE Systems HAWK T2

Role: Advanced fast-jet training aircraft for RAF, RN and RM pilots
Engine: 1 x Rolls Royce Adour 951 FADEC/turbofan delivering 6,500lb of thrust
Length: 41' **Wingspan:** 32' 7" **Height:** 13' 1"
Max. Weight: 20,000lb **Max. Speed:** Mach 1 at altitude **Crew:** 1 or 2 pilots
Avionics: Two mission computers host simulations of sensor and weapons systems; a data link allows synthetic radar inputs for intercept training and synthetic electronic warfare threats. Inertial and GPS navigation systems.
Armament: 7 hardpoints capable of carrying a total of 6,800lb of weapons, including 1 x 30mm cannon pod on centreline, AIM-9 Sidewinder or ASRAAM missiles and bombs.

Squadron Service: 4(R) Squadron Royal Air Force

Notes: 4 (Reserve) Squadron forms part of Number 4 Flying Training School at RAF Valley within the Military Flying Training System and provides advanced fast-jet training for RAF, RN and RM pilots up to the standard required for conversion onto operational types. The Hawk T 2 has a 'glass cockpit' with 3 full-colour, multi-function displays, similar to those in the Typhoon and F-35B, which display navigation, weapons and system information intended to immerse student pilots into a complex, data-rich tactical flying environment from the outset rather than just learning to fly the aircraft.

Short TUCANO T1

Role: Basic fast-jet training aircraft for RAF, RN and RM pilots
Engine: 1 x Garrett TPE 331-12B turboprop delivering 1,100 shp
Length: 32' 4" **Wingspan:** 37' **Height** 11' 2"
Max. Weight: 7,220lb **Max. Speed:** 300 knots **Crew:** 1 or 2 pilots
Avionics: Standard communications fit
Armament: None

Squadron Service 72(R) Squadron Royal Air Force

Notes: Operated by 72 (Reserve) Squadron as part of Number 1 Flying Training School at RAF Linton-on-Ouse, an element of the Military Flying Training System, the Tucano provides basic training for student RAF, RN and RM fast-jet pilots and RAF weapons system operators; it handles like a jet aircraft but is significantly cheaper to operate. Ascent plans to replace the Tucano with the Beechcraft T-6C Texan II in 2019.

Beech AVENGER T1

Role: Observer training
Engines: 2 x Pratt & Whitney PT6A-60A, each developing 1,050 shp
Length: 46' 8" **Wingspan:** 57' 11" **Height:** 14' 4"
Max. Weight: 15,000lb **Max. Speed;** 313 knots
Crew: 1 or 2 pilots, 4 student observers plus instructors
Avionics: Surface search and ground mapping radar
Armament: None

Squadron Service: 750 Naval Air Squadron

Notes: Avengers are civil-owned but military registered and used by 750 NAS at RNAS Culdrose as part of the MFTS. They provide Phase 3 training for RN observers and lead-in training for RAF AWACS systems operators. Phases 1 and 2 of the Observer Course are carried out by 703 Squadron at RAF Barkston Heath.

CROWN COPYRIGHT/MOD

Airbus JUNO HT1

Role: Basic helicopter training
Engines: 2 x Turbomeca Arrius 2B, each developing 708 shp
Length: 39' 7" **Rotor diameter:** 33' 5" **Height:** 12' 4"
Max. Weight: 6,570lb **Max. Speed:** 140 knots
Crew: 2 pilots plus up to 6 passengers
Avionics: Defensive aids simulator; L-3 Wescam electro/optical camera
Armament: None

Squadron Service: 705 Squadron MFTS

Notes: The Juno HT1 began flying training at the Defence Helicopter School at RAF Shawbury in April 2018, replacing the Squirrel HT1. With twin engines and a night-vision goggle compatible glass cockpit, the new helicopter gives student pilots a better lead-in to operational types such as the Merlin and Wildcat than its predecessors. All 29 Junos are fitted with a defensive aids simulator operated by the instructor and wired for an electro/optical camera installation although at any one time only 10 will be so fitted with the aim of teaching students to operate, rather than just fly modern aircraft types.

● LEE HOWARD

Eurocopter AS365N DAUPHIN 2

Role: Passenger movement and training support
Engines: 2 x Turbomeca Arriel 2C each developing 838 shp
Length: 39' 9" Rotor diameter: 39' 2" Height: 13' 4"
Max. Weight: 9,480lb Max. Speed: 155 knots Crew: 1 or 2 pilots plus up to 11 passengers
Avionics: None
Armament: None

Notes: Similar to the H-65 helicopters operated by the US Coast Guard, 2 of these civil-owned military-registered, COMR, helicopters are operated for the RN by Bond Helicopters under contract. They are maintained at Newquay airport and used to support FOST in the sea areas off Plymouth. They are commonly tasked to transfer passengers between ships at sea but can also undertake a wide variety of other roles. On a day-to-day basis they fly from an operating facility within Devonport Naval base from which FOST staff can be flown from their headquarters directly to ships at sea.

Sea Launched Missiles

Trident II D5

The American built Lockheed Martin Trident 2 (D5) submarine launched strategic missiles are Britain's only nuclear weapons and form the UK contribution to the NATO strategic deterrent. 16 missiles, each capable of carrying up to 6 UK manufactured thermonuclear warheads (but currently limited to 4 under current government policy), can be carried aboard each of the Vanguard-class SSBNs. Trident has a maximum range of 12,000 km and is powered by a three stage rocket motor. Launch weight is 60 tonnes, overall length and width are 13.4 metres and 2.1 metres respectively.

Tomahawk (BGM-109)

This is a land attack cruise missile with a range of 1600 km and can be launched from a variety of platforms including surface ships and submarines. Some 65 of the latter version were purchased from America to arm Trafalgar-class SSNs with the first being delivered to the Royal Navy for trials during 1998. Tomahawk is fired in a disposal container from the submarine's conventional torpedo tubes and is then accelerated to its subsonic cruising speed by a booster rocket motor before a lightweight F-107 turbojet takes over for the cruise. Its extremely accurate guidance system means that small targets can be hit with precision at maximum range, as was dramatically illustrated in the Gulf War and Afghanistan. Total weight of the submarine version, including its launch capsule is 1816 kg, it carries a 450 kg warhead, length is 6.4 metres and wingspan (fully extended) 2.54 m. Fitted in Astute & T class submarines. It was announced in 2014 that the US Navy are to stop procuring the missile in 2015 which has implications for the production line, although an MoD spokesman expected this not to impact on UK requirements.

Harpoon

The Harpoon is a sophisticated anti-ship missile using a combination of inertial guidance and active radar homing to attack targets out to a range of 130 km, cruising at Mach 0.9 and carrying a 227 kg warhead. It is powered by a lightweight turbojet but is accelerated at launch by a booster rocket. Fitted to Type 23 frigates and four Type 45 destroyers. Harpoon was planned to be retired from Royal Navy service at the end of 2018, without replacement but this decision has now been deferred.

Sea Viper (Aster 15/30)

Two versions of the Aster missile equip the Type 45 Destroyer, the shorter range Aster 15 and the longer range Aster 30. The missiles form the weapon component of the Principal Anti Air Missile System (PAAMS). Housed in a 48 cell Sylver Vertical Launch system, the missile mix can be loaded to match the ships requirement. Aster 15 has a range of 30 km while Aster 30 can achieve 100 km. The prime external difference between the two is the size of the booster rocket attached to the bottom of the missile. PAAMS is known as Sea Viper in RN service.

Sea Wolf

Short range rapid reaction anti-missile and anti-aircraft weapon. The complete weapon system, including radars and fire control computers, is entirely automatic in operation. Type 23 frigates carry 32 Vertical Launch Sea Wolf (VLS) in a silo on the foredeck. Basic missile data: weight 82 kg, length 1.9 m, wingspan 56 cm, range c.5-6 km, warhead 13.4 kg. The VLS missile is basically similar but has jettisonable tandem boost rocket motors. The Sea Wolf system is gradually being replaced by Sea Ceptor.

Sea Ceptor

Incorporating the Common Anti-Air Modular Missile (CAMM) family, being developed to replace the Rapier and Sea Wolf SAM systems, plus the ASRAAM short range Air-to-Air Missile. It will arm the Royal Navy's Type 23 frigates and its Type 26 Global Combat Ships. In Spring 2012 the MoD awarded MBDA UK a five-year Demonstration Phase contract worth £483 million to develop the missile for the RN. In September 2013 a £250 million contract was announced to manufacture the missile in the UK, sustaining around 250 jobs at MBDA sites in Stevenage, Filton and Lostock. Installation of the Sea Ceptor on Type 23 frigates started in 2015 with ARGYLL and the last will be completed by 2021. CAMM missiles will be fitted in the existing VL Sea Wolf silo (one canister per cell for a maximum of 32 missiles).

Guns

114mm Vickers Mk8 Mod 1

The Royal Navy's standard medium calibre general purpose gun which arms the Type 23 frigates and Type 45 destroyers. The Mod 1 is an electrically operated version of the original gun and is recognised by its angular turret. First introduced in 2001 it is now fitted in all Type 23 and Type 45 vessels. Rate of fire: 25 rounds/min. Range: 22,000 m. Weight of Shell: 21 kg.

Phalanx

A US-built CIWS designed around the Vulcan 20 mm rotary cannon. Rate of fire is 3000 rounds/min and effective range is c.1500 m. Fitted in Type 45 and some Wave, Bay and Fort classes. Block 1B began entering service from 2009. Incorporates side mounted forward looking infra-red enabling CIWS to engage low aircraft and surface craft. In October 2012 it was announced that a further five Phalanx Block 1B mountings were to be procured to protect RFA ships.

DS30B 30mm

Single mounting carrying an Oerlikon 30mm gun. Fitted to Type 23 frigates and various patrol vessels and MCMVs. In August 2005 it was announced that the DS30B fitted in Type 23 frigates was to be upgraded to DS30M Mk 2 to include new direct-drive digital servos and the replacement of the earlier Oerlikon KCB cannon with the ATK Mk 44 Bushmaster II 30 mm gun. Consideration is already being given to purchasing additional DS30M Mk 2 systems for minor war vessels and auxiliaries.

GAM BO 20mm

A simple hand operated mounting carrying a single Oerlikon KAA 200 automatic cannon firing 1000 rounds/min. Maximum range is 2000 m. Carried by most of the fleet's major warships except the Type 23 frigates.

20mm Mk.7A

The design of this simple but reliable weapon dates back to World War II but it still provides a useful increase in firepower, particularly for auxiliary vessels and RFAs. Rate of fire 500-800 rounds/min.

Close Range Weapons

In addition to the major weapons systems, all RN ships carry a variety of smaller calibre weapons to provide protection against emerging terrorist threats in port and on the high seas such as small fast suicide craft. In addition it is sometimes preferable, during policing or stop and search operations to have a smaller calibre weapon available. Depending upon the operational environment ships may be seen armed with varying numbers of pedestal mounted General Purpose Machine Guns (GPMG). Another addition to the close in weapons is the Mk 44 Mini Gun, a total of 150 of which have been procured from the United States as a fleetwide fit. Fitted to a naval post mount, the Minigun is able to fire up to 3,000 rounds per minute, and is fully self-contained (operating off battery power).

Torpedoes

Sting Ray

A lightweight anti-submarine torpedo which can be launched from ships, helicopters or aircraft. In effect it is an undersea guided missile with a range of 11 km at 45 knots or 7.5 km at 60 knots. Length 2.1 m, diameter 330 mm. Type 23s have the Magazine Torpedo Launch System (MTLS) with internal launch tubes. Sting Ray Mod 1 is intended to prosecute the same threats as the original Sting Ray but with an enhanced capability against small conventionally powered submarines and an improved shallow-water performance.

Spearfish

Spearfish is a submarine-launched heavyweight torpedo which has replaced Tigerfish. Claimed by the manufacturers to be the world's fastest torpedo, capable of over 70 kts, its sophisticated guidance system includes an onboard acoustic processing suite and tactical computer backed up by a command and control wire link to the parent submarine. Over 20ft in length and weighing nearly two tons, Spearfish is fired from the standard 21-inch submarine torpedo tube and utilises an advanced bi-propellant gas turbine engine for higher performance. To undergo a £270 million upgrade which will include a new warhead, a change to the fuel system to improve safety, full digitisation of the weapon and a new fibre optic guidance link to improve performance. The work is to be carried out by BAE Systems at Portsmouth with deliveries beginning in 2020 and continuing to 2024.

Future Weapons

Sea Venom

Formerly known as the Future Anti-Surface Guided Weapon (Heavy), Sea Venom is a high-subsonic 'drop-launch' missile in the 110 kg-class incorporating an imaging infrared seeker (with provisions for an additional semi-active laser guidance channel), a two-way datalink for operator-in-the-loop control, and a 30kg warhead. Designed by MBDA to replace the helicopter air-launched Exocet, the missile will have a range of up to 25 km and will be able to counter targets up to corvette size. The FASGW programme, comprising both Heavy and Light missiles, is a joint venture between the UK and France. The missile will equip the RNs Wildcat helicopter. In July 2014, AgustaWestland received a £90 million contract to integrate the respective variants for deployment from the Wildcat HMA2. Each aircraft will be able to carry four missiles and it is anticipated that Initial Operating Capability will be achieved in 2020.

Martlet

Formerly known as the Future Anti-Surface Guided Weapon (Light), this missile is designed to counter small boat and fast inshore attack craft threats. It is based on the laser beam-riding variant of the Thales Lightweight Multi-role Missile (LMM). With a range of up to 8 km it carries a 3 kg blast fragmentation/shaped charge warhead travelling at about Mach 1.5. Missiles will be carried in a five-round launcher (with each Wildcat able to carry up to four launchers). Alternatively a mix of two Sea Venom on the outer pylon and two five round Martlet on the inner weapons station can be carried. An active laser guidance unit integrated within the L-3 Wescam nose turret will support laser beam-riding guidance. Trials of both variants of FASGW are planned to take place between late 2018 to late 2019.

Future Cruise/Anti-ship Weapon

The UK and France have signed an agreement to explore future missile technologies with MBDA which covers a three-year concept phase to develop future long range weapons for the British and French Navies and Air Forces. Each country will contribute EUR50 million to this phase. The Future Cruise/Anti-Ship Weapon programme will look at options to replace and improve existing Naval and Air Force weapons systems in the next decade. The new generation missiles will be a successor to the Harpoon, SCALP and Storm Shadow. The FC/ASW (future cruise/anti-ship weapon) programme's aim is to have, by around 2030, a new generation of missiles.

At the end of the line ...

Readers may well find other warships afloat which are not mentioned in this book. The majority have fulfilled a long and useful life and are now relegated to non-seagoing duties. The following list gives details of their current duties:

Pennant No	Ship	Remarks
D23	BRISTOL	Type 82 Destroyer - Sea Cadet Training Ship at Portsmouth.
M29	BRECON	Hunt Class Minehunter - Attached to the New Entry Training Establishment, HMS RALEIGH, Torpoint, as a static Seamanship Training Ship.
M103	CROMER	Single Role Minehunter - Attached to BRNC, Dartmouth as a Static Training Ship.
L3505	SIR TRISTRAM	Refitted as a Static Range Vessel at Portland.
S50	COURAGEOUS	Nuclear-powered Submarine - On display at Devonport Naval Base. Can be visited during Base Tours. Tel: 01752 552326 for details.
C35	BELFAST	World War II Cruiser Museum ship - Pool of London. Open to the public daily. Tel: 020 7940 6300
D73	CAVALIER	World War II Destroyer & Oberon class Submarine
S17	OCELOT	Museum Ships at Chatham. Open to the public. Tel: 01634 823800
S67	ALLIANCE	Submarine - Museum Ship at Gosport Open to the public daily. Tel: 023 92 511349
LCT7074	LANDFALL	A D-Day veteran. Refloated in October 2014 six years after she sank at Birkenhead. Undergoing restoration by the NMRN at Portsmouth. Eventually to be displayed outside the D-Day Museum, Southsea.
M1115	BRONINGTON	Sank at Birkenhead, its future now uncertain.
	BRITANNIA	Ex Royal Yacht at Leith. Open to the public.
	CAROLINE	Light Cruiser and veteran of the Battle of Jutland preserved at Belfast.
	M33	Coastal Monitor and veteran of the Gallipoli Campaign on display at Portsmouth as part of the National Museum of the Royal Navy.

Former HMS Ocean

Since the previous edition the following vessels were sold, disposed of
or are in long term storage and/or awaiting scrap:

OCEAN: The Landing Platform Helicopter ship was sold to Brazil and renamed ATLANTICO. She departed Portsmouth in June 2018. With no replacement it is envisaged that one of the Queen Elizabeth-class carriers will undertake the LPH role as required.

GLEANER: Small inshore survey craft used for the collection of data from the shallowest inshore waters. Her replacement, MAGPIE, will be the largest of 38 new workboats being supplied to the MoD by Atlas Elektronik.

SEA KING Helicopter: The last 7 Sea Kings in RN service were operated by 849 NAS. At the end of September 2018, after almost 50 years of active operations, they left RNAS Culdrose for retirement. 'Crowsnest' Merlin HM2s are intended to replace Sea Kings gradually between 2018 and 2020.

At the time of writing (February 2019) the following ships
were laid up in long term storage or awaiting sale:

PORTSMOUTH: ATHERSTONE; QUORN; DILIGENCE; WALNEY; BLACK ROVER; GOLD ROVER.

PLYMOUTH: TORBAY; TIRELESS; TRAFALGAR; TURBULENT; SCEPTRE; SUPERB; SPLENDID; SPARTAN; SOVEREIGN; CONQUEROR; VALIANT; WARSPITE.

ROSYTH: RESOLUTION; RENOWN; REPULSE; REVENGE; SWIFTSURE; CHURCHILL; DREADNOUGHT.